Chicken
Chicken
Chicken

Notes

1. Standard level spoon measurements are used in all recipes.
1 tablespoon = one 15 ml spoon
1 teaspoon = one 5 ml spoon

2. Both standard and metric measurements have been given in all recipes. Use one set of measurements only and not a mixture of both.

3. Eggs should be medium unless otherwise stated. The Food and Drug Administration and the USDA Food Safety and Inspection Service advise that eggs should not be consumed raw. This book contains dishes made with raw or lightly cooked eggs. It is prudent for more vulnerable people such as pregnant and nursing mothers, invalids, the elderly, babies, and young children to avoid uncooked or lightly cooked dishes made with eggs. Once prepared, these dishes should be kept refrigerated and used promptly.

4. Chicken should always be cooked thoroughly and should be tested with a skewer at the end of cooking time to ensure juices run clear.

5. Whole milk should be used unless otherwise stated.

6. Fresh herbs should be used unless otherwise stated. If unavailable, use dried herbs as an alternative but halve the quantities stated.

7. Ovens should be pre-heated to the specified temperature – if using a convection oven, follow manufacturer's instructions for adjusting the time and the temperature.

8. Pepper should be freshly ground black pepper unless otherwise stated.

9. This book includes dishes made with nuts and nut derivatives. It is advisable for readers with known allergic reactions to nuts and nut derivatives and those who may be potentially vulnerable to these allergies, such as pregnant and nursing mothers, invalids, the elderly, babies, and children, to avoid dishes made with nuts and nut oils. It is also prudent to check the labels of pre-prepared ingredients for the possible inclusion of nut derivatives.

10. Vegetarians should look for the "V" symbol on a cheese to ensure it is made with vegetarian rennet. There are vegetarian forms of Parmesan, Feta, Cheddar, Cheshire, dolcelatte, and many goats' cheeses, among others.

11. Egg symbols indicate the degree of difficulty for each recipe, with one egg being the simplest.

Laurence & Gilles Laurendon

Chicken
Chicken
Chicken

Photographs by Akiko Ida & Laurent Parrault

ici
la
PRESS

One day, a hen wanted to leave the poultry farm where she was kept.

"It's madness," shouted the farmer, "you'll get eaten by a fox, run over by a car, or insulted left, right and center. You'll just be mocked and humiliated."

The hen wouldn't hear any of it and so she left.

She only just escaped being eaten by a fox, she was almost run over by a car, people said all around her how stupid she was, and she was mocked and insulted on every side.

When she returned, she said to the farmer:

"You were right. I only just escaped being eaten by a fox and run over by a car and everybody made fun of me."

"I told you," said the farmer triumphantly.

"Yes, but you didn't tell me everything," said the angry hen. "There's worse than that!"

"What?" said the farmer, surprised.

"They're writing a book about us!"

"A book about hens," chuckled the farmer. "If you think I'm going to swallow that!"

"They are, really," said the hen. "And in this book they even say that hens are intelligent, beautiful, brave, and...excellent to eat."

The farmer burst out laughing!

"A book about hens – but who would read such a thing! I see you haven't lost your taste for concocting stories, little hen."

The little hen seemed offended.

"Well, if you don't believe me, ask the other hens! Let us all go off together and ask us when we come back. Then you'll see!"

The farmer opened wide the doors of the henhouse with tears of laughter streaming down his face.

A book about hens! Whatever next!

He never saw them again!

The good
layers

Traveling hens

Hens have the reputation of being cowardly, chicken-hearted, and so stupid that they throw themselves under the wheels of cars. They are considered only good for laying eggs, hatching them, and bringing up a brood of cheeky chicks. They live helplessly in their henhouse, secluded in their enclosure.

Nothing could be further from the truth! The hen is, on the contrary, an intrepid traveler. And as she is intelligent (her IQ being well above that of other feathered creatures), she limits her efforts to the strict minimum. Rather than embark upon dangerous migrations across continents like stupid geese or vain gulls, she prefers...to hitchhike. Thus it was that she shared in the adventures of the great explorers.

At sea, the hen was precious: she provided the crew with fresh eggs. And when she put feet on dry land again, it didn't take her long to breed generations of clucking hens. Yellow ones, white ones, speckled ones, black ones, blue ones...the hen is a model of tolerance who knows how to mix with others. We should take our lead from her!

On land, she adapted to any climate and all situations. Some hens followed Marco Polo in his travels, others knew Jacques Cartier or Genghis Khan. Christopher Columbus was eternally grateful to them. La Pérouse was happy to find some on Easter Island. The more sporty ones did not sneer at joining the long desert caravans. And do you know that these intrepid fowls even conquered space before man did? Yes, you have read correctly: in 1793, for the first time in history, living beings were able to fly in a hot-air balloon. These three honorable aeronauts, pioneers in the conquest of space, were a sheep, a duck, and...a cock! (All right, it's not a hen, but even so!) Enough to silence those who say slanderous things about hens, taking them for "simple, silly creatures" (Bossuet).

Araucana

identity tag

She is called "the hen with green eggs" on account of her beautiful eggs, which are a lovely celadon green color. Originally from Chile, the araucana is very common in Latin America but also in the United States and the Caribbean.

cock: 4 to 5 lb. (2 to 2.5 kg)
hen: 3 to 4 lb. (1.6 to 2 kg)
egg: 2 oz. (55 g), green
varieties: golden, blue, black, cuckoo, white...

Pirate's chicken with coconut milk

For pirates, chicken presented the opportunity for a proper celebration meal to mark the taking of a schooner or the capture of a galleon. It was a feast reserved for fair weather days. On stormy days, there was no point in calling up the master chicken chef: the rolling of the ship would have overturned his cooking pot! Chicken broke the monotony of meals made up of dry biscuits, meat, or dried fish! This recipe is a memento of those far-off epic days.

Serves 4 to 5
Preparation: 20 minutes/Cooking: 45 minutes
Degree of difficulty:

1½ lb. (750 g) fresh spinach leaves
3 tbsp. sunflower oil
1 tbsp. water
1 small oven-ready chicken, about 2½ lb. (1.25 kg), cut up
1 onion, chopped
1 garlic clove, chopped
1 in. (2.5 cm) piece of fresh ginger root, peeled and grated
1¼ cups (300 ml) chicken stock
1 cup (250 ml) coconut milk
Salt and freshly ground black pepper
Desiccated or freshly grated coconut, to garnish (optional)

Carefully wash the spinach and take off the stalks and any woody bits. Heat 1 tbsp. oil in a pot and add the spinach. Add the measured water and some salt and cook over a fairly high heat, stirring once or twice. Add a small amount of pepper, cover, and leave to cook for 5 minutes.

Season the chicken pieces all over; set aside. Heat the remaining oil in a separate pan, add the onion, and sauté until lightly browned. Add the garlic and ginger and sauté for 1 minute.

Add the chicken pieces and fry them until lightly browned all over. Add the spinach mixture and chicken stock and stir to mix. Cover and cook gently for about 20 minutes.

Finally, pour in the coconut milk, cover, and cook gently for another 5 to 10 minutes, or until the chicken is cooked and tender. Garnish with coconut, if using, and serve with boiled white rice.

Saffron chicken

This recipe comes to us from the islands of Cape Verde, where the cooking has been influenced by both Africa and Portugal. This chicken stew is a traditional dish there. It is simple and tasty.

Serves 4 to 6
Preparation: 20 minutes/Cooking: 2¾ hours
Degree of difficulty:

1 oven-ready chicken, about 3 lb. (1.5 kg), cut up
2 tbsp. sunflower oil
2 onions, finely chopped
2 garlic cloves, finely chopped
3 tbsp. chopped ripe tomatoes
3 carrots, thinly sliced
½ tsp. saffron strands
1 cup (250 ml) water
3 potatoes, cut into large cubes
1 small fresh green or red chili, left whole
1 bay leaf
Salt and freshly ground black pepper
Fresh bay leaf, to garnish

Season the chicken pieces all over with salt and pepper, then set aside. Heat the oil in a flameproof casserole dish, add the onions and garlic, and sauté for 5 minutes. Add the chicken pieces and cook until well browned all over, turning occasionally.

Add the tomatoes, carrots, saffron, and measured water. Bring to the boil, then reduce the heat, cover, and simmer gently for 1¼ hours. Stir occasionally and, if necessary, add a little extra water to the casserole.

Add the potatoes, chili, and bay leaf. Cover and cook very gently for another 1¼ hours, or until the chicken is cooked and tender.

Taste and adjust the seasoning, if necessary. Remove and discard the chili and bay leaf. When serving, crush 2 or 3 of the potato cubes in the cooking juices to thicken the sauce. Serve very hot, garnished with a fresh bay leaf.

Saffron chicken

Masala chicken

Réunion

Masala chicken

A great classic of Creole cuisine!
Masala is a mixture of spices originally used in Indian cooking. The Indians brought it with them when they came to inhabit the island of Réunion. It is usually made up of peppers, curry leaves, cumin, cloves, coriander, fenugreek, mustard, and aniseed... the "authentic recipe" for masala doesn't exist!
It varies from one village to the next, from one family to another, and is the subject of endless discussions.
From this recipe, you will also be able to create a delicious masala of pork or lamb. The basic principle is the same! If you are not able to find masala, use garam masala.

Serves 4 to 6
Preparation: 20 minutes/Cooking: 50 minutes

Degree of difficulty:

2 tbsp. sunflower oil
1 small oven-ready chicken, about 2½ lb. (1.25 kg), cut up
1 onion, finely chopped
3 garlic cloves, finely chopped
1 in. (2.5 cm) piece of fresh ginger root, peeled and grated
1 fresh thyme sprig
7 oz. (200 g) tomatoes, skinned and chopped
2 tbsp. masala powder (or garam masala)
1¼ cups (300 ml) chicken stock
Salt and freshly ground black pepper
Fresh herb sprigs, to garnish

Heat the oil in a heavy bottomed pan, add the chicken pieces, and cook over a fairly high heat until browned all over, turning occasionally.

Add the onion, garlic, ginger, and thyme sprig and sauté for 1 minute. Add the tomatoes, masala powder, and seasoning, then stir in the chicken stock.

Bring to a boil, then reduce the heat, cover and cook over low heat for about 40 minutes or until the chicken is cooked and tender. Check and adjust the seasoning, if necessary. Garnish with fresh herb sprigs and serve with boiled rice and pickled vegetables.

West Indies

Pattypan squash with quinoa, diced chicken, and pineapple

The pattypan squash is one of the oldest vegetables grown. Round, with a pale green skin, it has, like the pumpkin and other numerous varieties of marrow, found its ideal habitat in the Caribbean. In this dish, the little squashes look wonderfully delicate and are a feast for the eye. Choose yellow ones for preference, because they are even brighter. Their lack of sweetness and their firm flesh go perfectly with the chicken and diced pineapple. Quinoa, which is an herbaceous plant of the Andes grown for its nutritious seeds, is available in some supermarkets, health food shops, and specialty food shops.

Serves 4
Preparation: 25 minutes/Cooking: 35 minutes

Degree of difficulty:

1 tbsp. sunflower oil
½ cup (125 g) quinoa
1 cup (250 ml) hot chicken stock
8 mini pattypan squash (or baby squash)
5 oz. (150 g) cooked skinless boneless chicken breast, cut into very small chunks
½ fresh pineapple, peeled, cored, and cut into very small chunks
Salt and freshly ground black pepper

Make sure you have a steamer ready and keep it to one side. Heat the oil in a heavy bottomed pot, add the quinoa, and stir to mix. Add the chicken stock and season lightly with pepper. Bring to a boil, then reduce the heat, cover, and cook over very low heat for about 15 minutes or until the quinoa is cooked and the stock has been absorbed.

Meanwhile, prepare the squash for cooking. Put some water on to heat in the steamer. Wash the squash. As soon as the water boils, place them in the top section of the steamer, cover, and leave to cook for 5 minutes.

Cut a little "hat" from the top of each squash and scoop out and discard the seeds with a small spoon.

In a bowl, mix the cooked quinoa mixture with the chicken and pineapple to make a stuffing and add seasoning to taste.

Spoon the stuffing into the squash, replace their "hats," and return them to the steamer. Cover and steam for about 10 minutes, or until tender. Serve warm.

Pattypan squash with quinoa,
diced chicken, and pineapple

Chicken with Bourbon vanilla

Réunion

Chicken with Bourbon vanilla

In former times, the island of Réunion was called "Bourbon Island." Vanilla plants were introduced there in 1819. A black slave carried out the first artificial insemination of the vanilla plants. Since then, Bourbon vanilla has become very acclimatized, and today it is considered to be among the best in the world. Here, the "black flower" infuses the chicken with its sweet, musky flavor. This chicken dish with vanilla is equally good cold.

Serves 6
Preparation: 25 minutes, plus resting
Cooking: About 1½ hours

Degree of difficulty:

2 Bourbon vanilla pods
1 oven-ready chicken, about 3 lb. (1.5 kg)
1 small carton, about 7 oz. (200 g),
  fromage blanc, whipped
1 bread roll
Salt and freshly ground black pepper

Prepare the chicken the day before: Split the vanilla pods lengthwise and carefully remove the precious seeds using the point of a knife.

Make cuts in the flesh and skin of the bird and gently slide the vanilla seeds underneath the skin, then rub the skin with the vanilla pods. Wrap the chicken in plastic wrap and let it rest in a cool place or the refrigerator for at least 24 hours.

Cut the vanilla pods into four, saving 2 pieces for garnish and mixing the rest with the *fromage blanc*. Cover and store in the refrigerator.

The following day, prepare your stuffing. In a blender or food processor, or by hand, make the bread roll into breadcrumbs. Blend with the vanilla-flavored *fromage blanc*.

Remove and discard the plastic wrap from the chicken. Season the inside of the chicken with salt and pepper, then stuff it with the *fromage blanc* breadcrumb mixture. Tie up the opening with ovenproof string and place the chicken in a roasting pan. Season all over with salt and pepper.

Place in a preheated 425°F (220°C) oven about 1¼ to 1½ hours or until the chicken is cooked and tender.

During cooking, every 15 minutes or so, baste the chicken with the cooking juices and give it a quarter turn, so that it becomes perfectly golden and infused with the flavors.

Carve and serve the chicken and stuffing with slices of fried banana or with steamed couscous. Garnish with the reserved vanilla pod pieces.

Chicken cari

Réunion
Chicken cari

On the island of Réunion, they like birds who wander about freely: country hens with long necks who stand tall and proud on their feet and lead a life that is wild and free. This gives their flesh such a tasty texture that they all finish up as a cari or a masala...even the fighting cocks! The basis of cari is a mixture of finely chopped onions, garlic, ginger, salt, and crushed pepper.
They also add curcumin (Indian saffron), tomato, and thyme. After that, anything is possible. It's up to you to improvise!

Serves 4 to 6
Preparation: 20 minutes/Cooking: 55 minutes

Degree of difficulty:

2 tbsp. peanut oil
1 small oven-ready chicken, about 2½ lb. (1.25 kg), cut up
4 onions, finely chopped
1 fresh thyme sprig
6 garlic cloves, crushed
1 in. (2.5 cm) piece of fresh ginger root, grated
1 tsp. curcumin
4 tomatoes, chopped
Salt and freshly ground black pepper

Heat the oil in a heavy bottomed pan. Add the chicken pieces and fry them quickly for a few minutes over a fairly high heat. When they are browned all over, remove them from the pan using a slotted spoon, place on a plate, and keep warm.

Add the onions and thyme to the pan and sauté for 5 minutes. Return the chicken to the pan, add the garlic and ginger, and season with curcumin. Stir and allow the flavors to gently combine, then reduce the heat a little to avoid anything sticking to the bottom of the pan.

Add the tomatoes and cook for 5 to 6 minutes, stirring occasionally. Add enough water to just cover the ingredients. Bring to a boil, then reduce the heat a little and cook, uncovered, for 25 to 30 minutes or until the chicken is cooked and tender. During this time the sauce will gradually reduce and thicken a little. Serve your cari chicken very hot accompanied by boiled rice.

Thailand
Thai chicken broth

Here is a recipe inspired by Thai cooking. The broth is delicately infused with the flavors of the ginger, lemongrass, coriander, and coconut milk.

Serves 4 to 6
Preparation: 15 minutes/Cooking: 35 minutes

Degree of difficulty:

2 lemongrass stalks
2⅓ cups (600 ml) chicken stock
2 onions, thinly sliced
1 garlic clove, finely chopped
1 in. (2.5 cm) piece of fresh ginger root, peeled and grated
2⅔ cups (400 ml) coconut milk
Juice of ½ lemon
2 tbsp. chopped fresh coriander
2 tbsp. nuoc nam (fish sauce)
Salt and freshly ground black pepper
Fresh coriander sprigs, to garnish

Wash and dry the lemon grass stalks, then cut them into small pieces; set aside.

In a saucepan, heat the chicken stock gently until almost boiling, then add the onions, garlic, ginger, and lemongrass. Bring to a boil, then reduce the heat, cover, and simmer for about 20 minutes.

Remove the pan from the heat, push the flavored broth through a sieve (or blend in a blender or food processor until smooth), and pour the mixture back into the rinsed-out pan. Stir in the coconut milk, bring gently to a boil, and simmer for another 5 minutes.

Stir in the lemon juice and chopped coriander, add the nuoc nam, then taste and adjust the seasoning. Ladle into soup bowls, garnish with coriander sprigs and serve immediately.

When hens had teeth

Hens have an ancestor in common with all birds: the archaeopteryx. This mysterious animal lived in the Jurassic period (150 million years ago for those who don't know!).

This feathered dinosaur, as big as a crow, had the teeth of a reptile! He seems to have been the precious missing link between the dinosaur and the bird. As for the domestic hen, if we are going to limit ourselves strictly to her family tree, the most distant relative is the bankiva or wild hen, of which there are four representatives still in existence: bankiva, La Fayette's junglefowl, Sonnerat's junglefowl, and java. It's difficult to say which of these sub-species was at the origin of our docile domestic hen.

Prehistory cannot enlighten us! Up to now, no hen fossils have been found in Europe. But we continue to search! The most ancient documents are to be found in China, where the hen is believed to have arrived in full flight (from India) around 1400 B.C., which is quite a number of generations ago!

Brahma

identity tag

This is a giant of the henhouse, her feathered feet sweeping the ground with ample and majestic movements. Originally from India, she conquered Europe in the 19th century.

cock: 7 lb. (3.5 kg)
hen: 6 to 8 lb.
(3 to 4 kg)
egg: 2 oz. (55 g),
tinted (from yellow
to reddish-brown)
varieties: speckled,
black, Columbian,
partridge, silver, blue,
white, cuckoo...

India

Mildly spiced chicken

Ginger brings a freshness and intensity to dishes, and is a truly healthy spice. You can serve this chicken dish with delicious Indian breads such as chapattis or parathas.

Serves 6
Preparation: 20 minutes/Cooking: 50 minutes
Degree of difficulty:

4 tsp. sunflower oil
1 onion, chopped
4 garlic cloves, chopped
1 tbsp. grated peeled fresh ginger root
1 small cinnamon stick
1 tsp. ground curcumin (Indian saffron)
¼ teaspoon freshly ground black pepper
1 tsp. ground cumin
2 tomatoes, cut into chunks
½ tsp. freshly ground cardamom seeds
1 small carton, about ⅔ cup (150 g), natural yogurt
Salt
1 oven-ready chicken, about 3 lb. (1.5 kg), cut up
⅔ cup (65 g) blanched almonds
Cooked basmati rice, to serve

Heat 3 tsp. oil in a heavy bottomed pan. Add the onion, garlic, and ginger and fry them all together for a few minutes. Add the cinnamon stick, curcumin, black pepper, and cumin. On contact with the heat, the flavors will develop and become more intense.

Add the tomatoes, ground cardamom, yogurt, and salt to taste. Stir, then cover and cook gently about 5 minutes. Add the chicken pieces, turning to coat them all over with the sauce. Cover and cook gently about 40 minutes or until the chicken is cooked and tender, checking from time to time that the sauce is not becoming too dry. If it is, add a little water.

While the chicken is cooking, heat the remaining oil in a heavy bottomed frying pan and fry the almonds in the oil until toasted all over. Remove the pan from the heat and set aside.

Prepare and cook some basmati rice, stir the almonds into the rice, and serve with the mildly spiced chicken.

India

Chicken with coriander and fresh ginger

Garam masala is at the heart of Indian cooking. This mixture of spices (cumin, coriander, cardamom, black pepper, cinnamon, nutmeg, and cloves) is easy to prepare yourself. You simply roast the spices separately, then grind them all together. A real delight, which will leave your kitchen with pungent aromas.

Serves 4 to 6
Preparation: 20 minutes, plus marinating/Cooking: 35 minutes
Degree of difficulty:

2 in. (5 cm) piece of fresh ginger root, peeled and grated
2 small bunches of fresh coriander, chopped
2 garlic cloves, chopped
1 tsp. paprika
1 tsp. garam masala
Juice of 2 lemons
1 small oven-ready chicken, about 2½ lb. (1.25 kg), cut up
2 tbsp. sunflower oil
4 very ripe tomatoes, cut into chunks
Salt and freshly ground black pepper
1 small bunch of fresh mint, chopped, to garnish

In a bowl, mix the ginger, chopped coriander, and garlic with the paprika, garam masala, and lemon juice. Put the chicken pieces into this marinade and turn to coat all over. Cover with plastic wrap and leave in a cool place about 6 hours.

Heat the oil in a heavy bottomed pan, add the chicken pieces and marinade, and fry over a fairly high heat for about 20 to 25 minutes, allowing the chicken to brown nicely all over. Add the tomatoes, season with salt and pepper, then cover and leave to simmer about 10 minutes, or until the chicken is cooked and tender.

Garnish with chopped mint and serve with boiled rice.

Mongolia

Mongolian stew

This convivial fondue is much appreciated in Mongolia and northern China. A stunning effect is guaranteed! Especially if you possess a proper fondue pot, that can sit on the table over a lighted flame while the broth simmers in it.

Serves 4
Preparation: 20 minutes/Cooking: 3 to 5 minutes
Degree of difficulty:

3½ oz. (100 g) fresh spinach
¼ Chinese cabbage, washed and finely shredded
1 small bunch of fresh coriander leaves
7 oz. (200 g) skinless boneless chicken breast, thinly sliced
7 oz. (200 g) beef fillet, thinly sliced
3 chicken livers, thinly sliced
8 oz. (250 g) tofu, cut into cubes
8 cups (2 l) chicken stock
Soy sauce, to taste
Salt and freshly ground black pepper

Rinse the spinach leaves, drain, then dry them in a tea towel and chop. Put them in a bowl and set aside. Put the cabbage in a separate bowl, and the coriander leaves in another bowl. Set aside.

Put the sliced meats and livers into 2 bowls and put the tofu into a separate bowl too.

Fill the fondue pot with chicken stock and set it over the flame in the center of the table. Heat the stock until hot. Season to taste with salt and pepper.

Present the bowls of meat, tofu and vegetables to your guests, who will then dip their ingredients into the hot stock. Ensure the meat is cooked thoroughly in the stock before eating. Season the cooked foods with soy sauce, if desired.

Sri Lanka

Hard-boiled eggs with coconut milk

This dish is both simple and tasty and very popular in southern India, Malaysia, and Sri Lanka, where we found this recipe. It involves a subtle blend of spices and coconut milk.

Serves 4 to 6
Preparation: 10 minutes/Cooking: 35 minutes
Degree of difficulty:

6 eggs
1 tbsp. sunflower oil
1 onion, chopped
1 garlic clove, chopped
1 in. (2.5 cm) piece of fresh ginger root, peeled and grated
½ tsp. ground curcumin (Indian saffron)
4 dried curry leaves (or 1 tbsp. curry powder)
1 small cinnamon stick
2 cups (500 ml) coconut milk
1 tsp. lemon juice
Salt

Begin by cooking the eggs. Put them in a saucepan of cold water, bring to a boil, and let them boil gently for 9 minutes. Rinse the boiled eggs under cold running water, then shell the eggs. Set aside.

Heat the oil in a heavy bottomed pan. Add the onion, garlic, and ginger and sauté until softened. Add the curcumin, curry leaves or powder, and cinnamon stick. Sauté for 2 minutes, stirring continuously, then stir in the coconut milk.

Add a little salt, then cover and leave to simmer for 10 to 12 minutes. Remove and discard the cinnamon stick and curry leaves. Stir in the lemon juice at the last minute.

Cut the hard-boiled eggs in half, arrange them on a plate and serve them covered with the warm coconut milk sauce, accompanied by plain basmati rice.

Hard-boiled eggs with coconut milk

The glorious chickens of Bresse

Blue feet, white plumage, red crest – the hens of Bresse are truly magnificent creatures! Free to roam, fed on corn and dairy products, their reputation is second to none. What's more, they benefit from the prestigious *"appellation d'origine contrôlée"* (AOC), a label which guarantees their quality.

Each year for more than a hundred and fifty years, the breeders of Bresse have organized big competitions between villages to nominate the most beautiful hens. The star is naturally the *poularde*, who only makes a brief appearance on French market stalls during the Christmas season. This queen of the hen run, with her exquisite meat, remains a luxury product.

Bresse

identity tag

One of the oldest
French breeds.
In Bresse, the
breeding zone
is strictly demarcated.

cock: 5 to 6 lb.
(2.5 to 3 kg)
hen: 4 to 5 lb.
(2 to 2.5 kg)
egg: 2½ to 3 oz.
(60 to 70 g), white
varieties: black, grey,
white, blue...

Light chicken liver soufflé

Light chicken liver soufflé

This light liver soufflé is made from the livers of Bresse poultry. They can be recognized by their lovely light pink color and are distinctive for their extraordinarily fine flavor. A word of advice for this recipe: don't open the oven door while it is cooking, otherwise the soufflé will collapse.

Serves 4
Preparation: 25 minutes/Cooking: 35 minutes
Degree of difficulty:

2 cups (500 ml) milk
7 oz. (200 g) brioche made with pure butter
4 light chicken livers from a Bresse chicken
 (or other chicken if Bresse is not available)
4 eggs, separated
Salt and freshly ground black pepper

Lightly butter a 7 in. (18 cm) soufflé or similar ovenproof dish and set aside. Warm the milk in a saucepan, then pour it over the brioche and let it soak in.

Rinse the chicken livers under cold running water, then carefully dry them with a cloth. Drain and discard the excess milk from the brioche and place the soaked brioche in the bowl of a blender or food processor. Add the chicken livers and egg yolks and blend together until well mixed. Alternatively, finely chop the livers and mix thoroughly with the egg yolks and soaked brioche.

In a separate bowl, whisk the egg whites until they stand in soft peaks, then fold them carefully into the egg yolk mixture. Season with salt and pepper.

Pour the mixture into the prepared soufflé dish. Place in a preheated oven at 350°F (180°C) about 35 minutes or until well-risen, golden brown, and just firm to the touch.

Serve the soufflé as soon as it comes out of the oven, accompanied by a tomato sauce.

Morel mushroom omelet

A classic recipe for springtime and a delicious souvenir of childhood days. Of course, this recipe is much better if you have gathered the morels yourself!

Serves 4
Preparation: 5 minutes/Cooking: 10 minutes
Degree of difficulty:

7 oz. (200 g) fresh morel mushrooms
1 tbsp. peanut oil
⅜ stick (40 g) butter
6 eggs
2 tbsp. water
Salt and freshly ground black pepper
Fresh herb sprigs, to garnish

First prepare the morels by washing them several times under cold running water and carefully wiping them with a cloth. If they are not too dirty, you can make do with brushing them lightly with a fine brush. Cut the morels in half and set aside.

Heat the oil and half the butter in a nonstick frying pan. Add the morels, season lightly with salt and pepper, and cook over low heat for several minutes, until browned. Remove the pan from the heat and allow the mushrooms to cool.

Break the eggs into a bowl, add the measured water, season with salt and pepper, and beat everything together well. Add the cooked morels.

Melt the remaining butter in the frying pan and pour in the egg mixture. Cook over a fairly high heat, stirring gently and drawing the mixture from the sides to the center as it sets, letting the liquid egg in the center run to the sides. When set, stop stirring and cook until the omelet is golden brown underneath and still creamy on top.

Slide the omelet onto a warmed plate and serve immediately, garnished with fresh herb sprigs.

Morel mushroom omelette

Chicken with red-clawed crayfish

The combination of crayfish and chicken is a wonderful one.
Years ago, this well-known specialty of the Lyons area was
prepared exclusively with "red-clawed" crayfish, which abounded
in the streams, rivers, and waterways. Now they are a rarity.
With or without them, this recipe is an amazing one. Certainly,
it demands a little time, but with what results!

Serves 4 to 6
Preparation: 45 minutes, plus resting
Cooking: 1 hour

Degree of difficulty:

1 oven-ready chicken weighing about
  3½ lb. (1.75 kg), cut up
2 tbsp. peanut oil
7 tbsp. (100 g) best-quality butter
2 carrots, sliced
2 onions, chopped
2 shallots, sliced
24 red-clawed crayfish with claws removed
2 cups (500 ml) dry white wine
⅓ cup (100 ml) chicken stock
¾ cup (200 ml) crème fraîche
4 tbsp. cognac
Pinch of paprika
Juice of 1 lemon
Salt and freshly ground black pepper

Season the chicken pieces generously with salt and pepper.
Heat the oil and ½ tbsp. (15 g) butter in a heavy bottomed pan.
Add the chicken pieces and cook until browned all over, turning
occasionally. Cover the pan and cook over low heat for about
15 minutes. Remove the pan from the heat and keep warm.

Melt tbsp. (15 g) butter in a second heavy bottomed pan,
add the carrots, and sauté until browned all over. Add the onions
and shallots and cook gently until they are transparent. Add the
crayfish and increase the heat. As soon as they begin to turn
red, add salt and pepper and pour in the wine and stock. Cover
and leave to boil for a few minutes, then turn off the heat.
After 5 minutes, take the crayfish out of the pan using a slotted
spoon, remove their tails, and put them to one side.

Crush the crayfish shells with a mortar and pestle. Mix in the
remaining butter, then add this crayfish butter to the cooking
juices in the pan and bring to a boil. Take the pan off the heat,
cover and leave to infuse for about 10 minutes. Strain the juice
through a piece of cheesecloth or a fine mesh china cap, pressing
hard on the carcasses to extract as much juice as possible. Leave
to rest for 20 minutes.

Carefully skim off the pink butter, which has formed on the
surface, and set aside. It will be useful for thickening your sauce.

Reduce the sauce by boiling it without a lid for a few minutes
then, away from the heat, add half the crème fraiche, the cognac,
and a pinch of paprika. Stir with a wooden spoon and then add
lemon juice and the remaining crème fraiche, stirring all the time.

Put back over very low heat (the crème fraiche must not boil),
swirl the pink butter into the sauce, and beat quickly.

Serve the chicken and crayfish coated with the sauce.

Chicken in half-mourning

This recipe was perfected by famous old mother Filloux, who used to cook different types of poultry in the same stock! A stock so concentrated that it became a veritable nectar! The term "half-mourning" simply comes from the black color of the slices of truffle inserted under the skin. This festive recipe – which only requires a little skill – is quite simply sublime!

Serves 6
Preparation: 25 minutes, plus resting
Cooking: 1 hour

Degree of difficulty:

1 oven-ready Bresse (or standard) chicken, about 3 lb. (1.5 kg)
1 truffle, thinly sliced
6 young carrots, washed
6 young leeks, washed
1 celery stick, roughly chopped
Salt and freshly ground black pepper

Prepare your bird the day before: Make little cuts in the skin around the thighs and fleshy parts. Carefully insert the truffle slices under the skin. Make sure they are evenly distributed so that the whole flesh is impregnated with the flavor. Wrap the chicken in a damp cloth and leave it to rest in a cool place or the refrigerator overnight.

The following day, place the chicken in a piece of cheesecloth and tie both ends with ovenproof string.

Put the carrots, leeks, celery, and seasoning in a heavy bottomed, ovenproof stew pot or casserole dish and half-fill it with water. Bring this to a boil and then plunge the chicken into it. Top off with water just to the level of the chicken.

Cover and cook over low heat for about 50 minutes or until the chicken is cooked and tender. Unwrap the chicken and carve into slices. Serve the chicken accompanied by the vegetables and a small dish of coarse salt.

Keep the cooking broth to make a sumptuous chicken and truffle-flavored risotto.

Thousand-year-old eggs!

Did you know about the eggs that are a thousand years old? They are a gourmet's delight, these mysterious objects from China. But these venerable eggs, sometimes called hundred-year eggs, are really only...a few months old!

The number, as in the best legends and fairy tales, only indicates how precious they are! For a long time they were kept solely for the emperor's table.

Coated in a thick mixture made of straw, clay, lime, tea leaves and aromatic plants, the eggs have "cooked" naturally inside their scented casing. When you break the shell, the egg is a beautiful shiny black color and the yolk is a delicate jade green.

When you taste it, there is no suspicious odor, just a sweet scent. Thousand-year-old eggs are traditionally eaten with ginger pickled in vinegar and soy sauce. So, if one day somebody presents you with this imperial delicacy, do not, whatever you do, offend your host: Don't wrinkle your nose, don't decline the offer, just savor it to the fullest! The promise of a thousand years of good eating is yours!

Cochin

identity tag

A giant hen originally from China, not from Cochin China as might be thought. She was imported into Europe (England) in 1843.

cock: 10 to 12 lb. (5 to 6 kg)
hen: 7 to 10 lb. (3.5 to 5 kg)
egg: tinted white
variety: partridge

Marbled eggs with
smoked China tea

China

Marbled eggs with smoked China tea

The marbled egg technique is very simple and the results are spectacular!

Serves 6
Preparation: 10 minutes, plus standing/Cooking: 5 minutes
Degree of difficulty:

6 eggs
2 cups (500 ml) spring water
4 tsp. smoked China tea
2 tbsp. soy sauce

Place the eggs in a saucepan of cold water, bring them to a boil, and let them boil gently for 9 minutes. Rinse them quickly under cold running water. Then, while the eggs are still lukewarm, crack the shells gently without shelling them. The simplest way to do this is to roll them on your worktop with the palm of your hand.

Now prepare the tea. Put the spring water in a saucepan and heat until it is just simmering. Remove the saucepan from the heat, add the tea leaves, and let it steep, covered, for 5 minutes. Add the soy sauce and the eggs and stir gently. Set aside for at least 1 hour before shelling the eggs, leaving them time to turn a pretty brown color.

Shell the eggs, cut them in half, and serve with a little salad of fresh herbs.

China

Chicken soup with fresh ginger

This Chinese soup is an authentic healthy broth! It was traditionally served to new mothers. It is in fact called "nursing mother's broth." Thanks to the highly nutritious qualities of the chicken stock and the tonic and antiseptic properties of the garlic and ginger, these young women quickly recovered their strength and energy.

Serves 4 to 6
Preparation: 10 minutes/Cooking: 35 minutes
Degree of difficulty:

4 cups (1 l) chicken stock
1 tbsp. sesame oil
2 garlic cloves, chopped
1 in. (2.5 cm) piece of fresh ginger root, peeled and grated
1 small oven-ready chicken, about 2½ lb. (1.25 kg), cut up
½ cup (125 ml) rice wine (or dry white wine)
2 tsp. soy sauce
Salt

Pour the stock into a saucepan and bring to a boil. Meanwhile, heat the oil in a wok, add the garlic and ginger, and stir-fry briefly until browned.

Add the chicken pieces and a little salt and stir-fry over fairly high heat for about 10 minutes, or until the chicken is well browned all over.

Add the hot chicken stock, put a lid on the wok, and leave to cook over gentle heat for about 15 minutes, or until the chicken is cooked and tender.

Pour in the rice wine and soy sauce, stir and leave to cook for a few more minutes. Serve very hot.

Chicken soup
with fresh ginger

Chicken salad with mint
and fresh coriander

Vietnam

Chicken salad with mint and fresh coriander

The mixture of cool salad and lukewarm chicken is a real success here. This recipe was inspired by our friend Maï, whose phô and Vietnamese-style grilled lobster are unforgettable.

Serves 4 to 6
Preparation: 15 minutes, plus marinating/Cooking: 10 minutes
Degree of difficulty:

2 onions, chopped
1 tbsp. soy sauce
1 lb. (500 g) skinless boneless chicken meat, cut into large cubes
1 tbsp. sunflower oil
2 tbsp. nuoc nam (fish sauce)
½ firm white cabbage, shredded
2 tbsp. chopped fresh mint leaves
2 tbsp. chopped fresh coriander leaves
Freshly ground black pepper
Fresh mint sprigs, to garnish

Mix together the onions and soy sauce in a bowl. Add the chicken pieces to this mixture and toss to coat all over, then set aside in a cool place for about 30 minutes.

Heat the oil in a wok, add the chicken and onions, and stir-fry over high heat for about 5 minutes, or until browned all over. Pour in the nuoc nam and lightly season with pepper. Stir-fry for a few minutes longer.

To prepare the salad: In a large bowl, mix the white cabbage with the chopped mint and coriander leaves. Arrange the chicken pieces over the salad, garnish with mint sprigs, and serve with boiled rice.

China

Piquant chicken soup

This great classic of Chinese cooking is a delicious way of using up chicken leftovers. For those who like very piquant soups, put a little pot of chili paste on the table!

Serves 4
Preparation: 15 minutes, plus standing/Cooking: 15 minutes
Degree of difficulty:

6 dried mushrooms such as morels or porcini
3½ oz. (100 g) bamboo shoots (use canned, if fresh are not available)
4 cups (1 l) chicken stock
7 oz. (200 g) plain tofu (dow foo), diced
1 cooked chicken breast, about 4 oz. (125 g), cut into thin strips
1 tbsp. rice wine (or dry white wine)
1 tbsp. soy sauce
2 tbsp. cornstarch
2 small fresh red chilies
1 fresh green chili
Salt and freshly ground black pepper
Fresh herb sprigs, to garnish

Put the mushrooms in a bowl, cover with lukewarm water, and leave to stand for 20 minutes. Meanwhile, rinse and drain the bamboo shoots, then cut them into thin slices. Drain the mushrooms and remove and discard the stalks, then cut the caps into thin strips.

Pour the chicken stock into a heavy bottomed pot and bring to a boil. Add the mushrooms, bamboo shoots, tofu, and chicken. Cook for 2 minutes, then add the rice wine and soy sauce.

Blend the cornstarch with a little cold water, then stir it into the soup. Heat gently, stirring continuously, until the soup thickens. Add the whole red and green chilies and leave to simmer for 5 minutes.

Taste, and add salt and pepper, if necessary. Remove and discard the chilies. Ladle into soup bowls, garnish with fresh herb sprigs, and serve hot.

Piquant chicken soup

China

Stir-fried chicken with soy and ginger

Thanks to its concave shape and high sides, the wok allows you to cook anything, even recipes with very precise timing. It is of great value in this very simple recipe which, in order to attain its full flavor, requires precise cooking.

Serves 4
Preparation: 15 minutes, plus marinating/Cooking: 12 minutes
Degree of difficulty:

1 tbsp. cornstarch
3 tbsp. soy sauce
1 tsp. granulated sugar
1 in. (2.5 cm) piece of fresh ginger root, peeled and grated
1 garlic clove, chopped
14 oz. (400 g) skinless boneless chicken breast,
 cut into small cubes
2 tbsp. sunflower oil
2 carrots, coarsely grated
4 oz. (125 g) bean sprouts
1 tbsp. chopped fresh coriander leaves
Salt and freshly ground black pepper
Fresh coriander sprigs, to garnish

Mix the cornstarch, soy sauce, and sugar with the ginger and garlic in a bowl. Add the chicken pieces to the marinade and stir until coated all over. Cover with plastic wrap and leave to rest in a cool place for 30 minutes. Strain the chicken and reserve the marinade.

Heat 1 tbsp. oil in a wok (or a frying pan), add the chicken pieces, and stir-fry for a few minutes, until seared all over. Push them to the sides of the wok.

Heat the remaining oil in the wok, add the carrots, and stir-fry for 2 to 3 minutes. Meanwhile, plunge the bean sprouts into a bowl of boiling water, leave for 1 minute, then drain. Add them to the wok.

Pour in the marinade, stir once, then leave to cook for about 5 minutes or until the chicken is cooked and tender. Season to taste with salt and pepper, then sprinkle the chopped coriander over the top. Garnish with coriander sprigs and serve immediately.

China

Shellfish soup with chicken broth

The abalone is a variety of sea-ear much prized in Chinese cooking, and it is indispensable in this recipe. It is a food reserved for feast days, and it can also be braised with shark fins. The combination of shellfish and chicken stock, although unusual, is delicious.

Serves 4
Preparation: 20 minutes, plus standing/Cooking: 15 minutes
Degree of difficulty:

2 oz. (50 g) dried mushrooms, such as porcini or morels
3½ oz. (100 g) bamboo shoots (use canned,
 if fresh are unavailable)
3 oz. (75 g) snow peas
4 cups (1 l) chicken stock
5 oz. (150 g) shelled abalone, cut into strips
2 tsp. rice wine (or dry white wine)
2 tsp. chili oil
1 tbsp. chopped fresh coriander leaves
Salt and freshly ground black pepper

Put the mushrooms in a bowl, cover with lukewarm water, and leave to stand for 20 minutes. Meanwhile, bring a small pan of water to a boil and immerse the bamboo shoots in the water. Leave for no more than 1 minute, then drain and rinse them under cold running water. Cut the bamboo shoots into thin slices.

Drain the mushrooms and remove and discard the stalks. Slice the mushroom caps thinly. Plunge the snow peas into a saucepan of boiling water to blanch, then drain and cut each one into 3 pieces.

Pour the chicken stock into a heavy bottomed pot and bring to a boil. Add the mushrooms, bamboo shoots, and abalone to the stock. Stir in the rice wine and seasoning, then cover and cook over very low heat for about 1 minute or until the abalone is just cooked. Stir in the snow peas and chili oil, then ladle into bowls. Sprinkle some chopped coriander over each portion and serve.

Shellfish soup
with chicken broth

China

Stir-fried chicken with snow peas

In China, cooking is very much linked to the lunar calendar. Traditionally, the cook chooses the food, utensils, and crockery according to the season. This recipe, with its crisp, fresh flavors, is one for the first days of spring.

Serves 2 to 3
Preparation: 20 minutes, plus marinating
Cooking: 6 to 7 minutes

Degree of difficulty:

10 oz. (300 g) small chicken breasts, cut into thin strips
7 tsp. rice wine (or dry white wine)
4 tsp. soy sauce
2 tbsp. peanut oil
1 onion, thinly sliced
1 handful of fresh chives, chopped
1 in. (2.5 cm) piece of fresh ginger root,
  peeled and finely chopped
5 oz. (150 g) snow peas
1 tsp. cornstarch
1 tbsp. water
Salt and freshly ground black pepper
Sesame oil, to serve
Cooked egg (optional) and fresh chives, to garnish

Arrange the chicken strips in a deep dish. Mix together 5 tsp. of rice wine and the soy sauce in a bowl, then pour this mixture over the chicken. Turn the chicken strips over in the marinade to cover completely. Cover with plastic wrap and set aside in a cool place for 20 minutes.

Heat the peanut oil in a wok, add the chicken and marinade and stir-fry for 2 to 3 minutes, or until the chicken is lightly browned all over. Remove the chicken strips from the wok, place on a plate, and keep warm.

Add the onion, chopped chives, and ginger to the wok and stir-fry for 1 minute. Add the snow peas, then return the chicken to the wok. Add the remaining rice wine and season lightly with salt and pepper.

Quickly mix the cornstarch with the measured water and pour into the wok, stirring all the time, until the mixture thickens. As you are serving, add a few drops of sesame oil to each portion. Garnish with cooked egg, if using, and fresh chives.

Vietnam

Chicken salad with garlic and ginger

You can also add a few strips of green papaya to this dish or try some bean sprouts cut into small pieces. These very long, slender, curved beans can be bought in Asian food shops and supermarkets.

Serves 4
Preparation: 20 minutes, plus marinating
Cooking: 8 minutes

Degree of difficulty:

1 in. (2.5 cm) piece of fresh ginger root,
 peeled and grated
1 garlic clove, chopped
2 tsp. nuoc nam (fish sauce)
1 tsp. granulated sugar
3 tbsp. peanut oil
2 chicken breasts, about 4 oz. (125 g) each,
 cut into thin slices
A few lettuce leaves
2 carrots, grated
5 oz. (150 g) bean sprouts
2 tbsp. chopped fresh coriander leaves

Prepare the marinade: Mix together the ginger, garlic, nuoc nam, sugar, and 2 tbsp. peanut oil in a small bowl. Put the chicken in a shallow dish and pour the marinade over the chicken. Toss to mix, then cover with plastic wrap and leave to stand in a cool place for 1 hour.

Arrange the lettuce leaves, carrots, and bean sprouts on a large plate.

Heat the remaining oil in a wok, add the chicken and marinade and stir-fry over fairly high heat for 6 to 8 minutes, or until the chicken is cooked and tender.

Arrange the chicken on top of the salad, drizzle the cooking juices over the top, and serve immediately, garnished with chopped coriander.

Chicken salad with garlic and ginger

"What beautiful eggs you have!"

In painting, sculpture, and music, the hen has often been scorned and despised: The pictures devoted to her are few and far between, and she normally only features as a detail in them. With the exception of original African and Oceanic art and artists like Itō Jakuchū or Picasso, the hen seems to be a subject reserved for the decoration of objects.

The cinema has been less unfair to her. The list is long of films containing references to our amiable gallinaceous friend: from *Chicken Run* to *Rabia my chick*, from *The Gold Rush* to *The Wing or the Leg*.

So, a bit of quiet there in the henhouse – they're filming!

identity tag

Created at the beginning of the last century by an enthusiast called Dr. Ramé, who took nearly thirty years to establish this hardy breed. Its name comes from the color of its plumage, which recalls that of the wood cuckoo.

cock: 7 lb. (3.5 kg)
hen: 6 lb. (3 kg)
egg: 2½ oz. (60 g), tinted
variety: cuckoo

Cuckoo of Rennes

Brittany

Chicken with Breton prune stuffing (*far breton*)

The idea is simple yet inspired: combining chicken with this classic Breton dish gives outstanding tenderness and flavor to the bird.

Serves 4 to 6
Preparation: 25 minutes
Cooking: 50 to 60 minutes
Degree of difficulty:

1¼ cups (300 ml) whole milk
⅛ stick (15 g) lightly salted butter,
  cut into small cubes
2 tbsp. all-purpose flour, sifted
½ oz. (15 g) granulated sugar
1 egg
5 prunes
¾ oz. (20 g) raisins
1 small oven-ready chicken,
  about 2½ lb. (1.25 kg)
Salt and freshly ground black pepper

First, prepare the stuffing. Heat the milk in a saucepan, stir in the butter, then remove the pan from the heat.

Mix the flour and sugar together in a bowl, then add the egg and beat together until mixed. Pour in the milk and melted butter, and continue to beat until well mixed.

Pour the mixture into a heavy bottomed saucepan and cook, uncovered, over gentle heat for several minutes, stirring continuously to avoid lumps forming. Remove the pan from the heat, stir in the prunes and raisins, then set aside until the mixture is lukewarm.

Stuff the chicken with this mixture, then truss it up using a needle and thread. Put the chicken in an ovenproof dish or roasting pan and season with salt and pepper. Place in a preheated 425°F (220°C) oven about 50 to 60 minutes, or until the chicken is cooked and tender. Baste regularly with the cooking juices during cooking. Serve the chicken and stuffing as soon as it comes out of the oven.

Chicken with Breton prune
stuffing (*far breton*)

Easter eggs

"The baby of the hen is the egg."
Raoul Lambert

The custom of Easter eggs is said to date back to the 4th century, when the Catholic Church forbade the faithful to eat eggs during Lent. As hens continued to lay, the eggs accumulated. What a lot of eggs! After forty days, they started to become a problem. What was to be done with them? It was from that time on that people adopted the habit of dyeing and decorating them and then giving them as presents. The tradition of Easter eggs was born.

In the eighteenth century, somebody had the idea (an expensive one for the time) of emptying the eggs and filling them with chocolate. It was a contest as to who could give the finest Easter egg. The daughter of Louis XV received eggs painted by Watteau. In Russia, the jeweller Fabergé created eggs made entirely of gold and precious stones for the czar. In the countries of central and eastern Europe, eggs were painted by hand with religious motifs or naïve scenes, which were supposed to bring good luck to the person who received them.

Nowadays, the egg tradition is still as flourishing and children eagerly await the moment for the "egg hunt." In France, it's the church bells that bring them, but in Britain and Germany rabbits bring them!

Naked-neck

identity tag

To be found in France on the Forez plain, but also in Réunion, Madagascar, Mauritius, and in many countries of eastern Europe (Transylvania). Not much liked because of her bare neck, she is nevertheless a *"grande dame"* of the farm with her own particular beauty.

cock: 5 to 6 lb. (2.5 to 3 kg)
hen: 4¾ to 5¾ lb. (2.4 to 2.8 kg)
egg: 2½ to 3 oz. (65 to 70 g), slightly tinted
varieties: black, white, cuckoo, red, Andalusian blue...

Golden soup

Chicken and beet soup (borscht)

Hungary

Golden soup

This soup owes its name to the orange color given to it by the saffron. In Jewish tradition, where food has great symbolic importance, chicken broth has a special place. It is the last dish served at the big meal that precedes Yom Kippur and it is presented for the Shabbat before the traditional boiled chicken.

Serves 4 to 6
Preparation: 20 minutes/Cooking: 2 hours

Degree of difficulty:

1 oven-ready chicken, about 3 lb. (1.5 kg)
2 carrots, sliced
2 leeks, washed and sliced
2 turnips, cut into large dice
1 celery stalk, cut into large chunks
1 tsp. saffron strands
1 bay leaf
3 onions, thinly sliced
1 small onion, with 3 cloves stuck into it
Salt and freshly ground black pepper

Put the chicken into a large, heavy bottomed pot and cover it with cold water, then add some salt. Bring to a boil, skim, and reduce the heat.

Cover and cook gently about 45 minutes, then add the carrots, leeks, turnips, and celery. Add the saffron, bay leaf, sliced onions, and clove-studded onion and cook over low heat, uncovered, for another hour or until the chicken is cooked and tender. Remove the chicken from the pot, set aside, and keep warm.

Remove and discard the bay leaf and clove-studded onion. Strain the broth and keep the vegetables warm. Taste and adjust the seasoning of the soup and ladle into soup bowls to serve.

Serve this soup as a starter or with the chicken and vegetables served alongside as a main course.

Russia

Chicken and beet soup (borscht)

This borscht is a classic of Russian Jewish cookery. It observes the rules of the Kashrut so it is prepared and served without cream.

Serves 4 to 6
Preparation: 25 minutes/Cooking: 2½ hours

Degree of difficulty:

1 oven-ready chicken, about 3 lb. (1.5 kg)
1 onion, with 2 cloves stuck into it
2 raw beets, cut into large chunks
2 carrots, thinly sliced
¼ white cabbage, thinly sliced
1 tbsp. wine vinegar
4 tbsp. tomato puree
1 tsp. granulated sugar
1 bay leaf
8 black peppercorns
4 potatoes
2 cups (600 ml) vegetable stock
Salt
2 tbsp. chopped fresh parsley, to garnish

Put the chicken and clove-studded onion into a large, heavy bottomed pot and cover with cold water. Bring to a boil, skim, then reduce the heat, cover, and cook gently for 1¾ hours. Remove and discard the clove-studded onion.

Add the beets, carrots, cabbage, wine vinegar, tomato puree, and sugar to the pot. Add the bay leaf and peppercorns together with a little salt, then cover and leave to simmer for 40 minutes.

Meanwhile, wash the potatoes and place them in a saucepan. Cover with the vegetable stock, bring to a boil, and cook until tender. Drain, cool slightly, then peel the potatoes and cut the flesh into large chunks. Keep warm.

Remove the chicken from the pot and cut the white meat into large chunks. Reserve any remaining meat for another recipe.

Remove and discard the bay leaf and peppercorns. Taste the chicken stock and adjust the seasoning if necessary, possibly adding a little more vinegar or sugar.

Put a few pieces of chicken into several large bowls, add the potatoes, and pour over the chicken broth with the vegetables.

Serve the borscht very hot, garnished with chopped parsley.

Moldavian meatballs

Children used to be told that this very simple recipe had the power to ward off evil spirits.

Serves 4
Preparation: 20 minutes/Cooking: 15 to 20 minutes
Degree of difficulty:

3½ oz. (100 g) day-old breadcrumbs
⅔ cup (150 ml) milk, heated until warm
13 oz. (400 g) skinless boneless chicken breast,
  very finely chopped or minced
1 large egg, beaten
2 tbsp. chopped fresh parsley
3 cups (750 ml) chicken stock
Salt and freshly ground black pepper
Fresh parsley sprigs to garnish

Put the breadcrumbs in a bowl and pour over the warm milk.

Season the chicken and put it into a large bowl with the egg and parsley. Squeeze the breadcrumbs, add them to the chicken and egg, and mix well. Shape the mixture into small round balls.

Gently heat the stock in a pan and as soon as it begins to simmer, add the chicken balls. Allow them to simmer, uncovered, for 10 to 15 minutes, or until thoroughly cooked.

Arrange the chicken balls on serving plates. Serve with a spicy tomato sauce accompanied by boiled rice and a bowl of the chicken broth. Garnish with parsley sprigs.

Chicken broth with vermicelli dumplings

This very homey recipe was prepared whenever there was some good chicken stock left in the house. As for making the vermicelli dumplings, it is simple and fun.

Serves 4 to 6
Preparation: 25 minutes/Cooking: 2¾ hours
Degree of difficulty:

1 oven-ready chicken, about 3 lb. (1.5 kg)
6 black peppercorns
1 fresh thyme sprig
1 bay leaf
2 carrots, thinly sliced
2 turnips, cut into chunks
¼ celery root, cut into large chunks
1 celery stalk, thinly sliced
1 leek, washed and thinly sliced
1 onion, chopped
1 small bunch of fresh parsley sprigs
Salt and freshly ground black pepper
Chopped fresh parsley, to garnish

For the vermicelli dumplings:
7 tbsp. flour
1 egg

Put the chicken into a large, heavy bottomed pot.
Cover with cold water and then bring to a boil over high heat.
Reduce the heat, skim, then add the peppercorns, salt, thyme, and bay leaf. Cover and cook over gentle heat for about 1¾ hours.

Add the carrots, turnips, celery root, celery, leek, onion, and parsley sprigs. Cover and continue to cook over low heat for another 45 minutes.

Remove the chicken from the pot and keep warm.
Push the stock through a sieve, then pour the liquid stock back into the pot and bring to a boil.

Make the vermicelli dumplings: Mix the flour and egg together in a bowl and season with salt and pepper. Immediately start dribbling this mixture into the boiling stock in the pot. Use a fork to help make it into "vermicelli." Leave to boil gently for 2 to 3 minutes or until cooked.

Carve the chicken and serve with a bowl of broth (stock) and the vermicelli dumplings. Garnish with chopped parsley at the last minute.

Chicken broth with
vermicelli dumplings

Chicken talk

Popular language has never been very kind to chickens and hens. Almost all the expressions in common use are disparaging toward them.

"Being chicken, chicken-livered, or chicken-hearted, chickening out, chickens coming home to roost (usually something devious from the past catching up), chicken feed (some paltry amount), running around like a headless chicken, henpecked…"

This unfavorable attitude finds expression in nearly all languages. As a Taoist hen might remark: "If what you have to say is no better than silence, then be quiet!"

The babble of Babel

A silly question: Is there one breed of hens that cock-a-doodles more than another? A Callas of the henhouse? "No," reply poultry breeders in unison. "They all sing in the same way." Except perhaps for wild hens, who are known for their sobriety. These quiet birds know that it's better not to attract Mr. Fox's attention too much. In fact, hens sing when they are laying eggs. But as some breeds lay more than others, it follows that some hens sing more. Q.E.D.

What do they sing? Well, on that point, nobody can agree. For the Germans, "The hen goes kikiriki." For the French, "She goes cot-cot-codec and coq cocorico!" "Not at all," say the Spaniards, "the cock goes quiquiriqui!" Which makes the British laugh because they know that the cock goes "cock-a-doodle-do!" In short, it's the tower of Babel. But we're all aware nowadays that diversity of language is one of the great benefits known to humanity!

Gallic dorée

identity tag

The oldest French breed. It has become France's national emblem, and the French cockerel lives perched on the tops of churches.

cock: 5 lb. (2.5 kg)
hen: 4 lb. (2 kg)
egg: 2 oz. (55 g), creamy white
variety: golden

Béarn

King Henry IV's chicken in the pot

"I want my good people to be able to put a chicken in the pot every Sunday," proclaimed Henry IV. The people of France listened to him. They've been preparing it since then for nearly four centuries! This famous recipe certainly wasn't invented by the good King Henry, but it's renowned because of him. By encouraging agriculture and breeding, Henry IV enabled the peasants, who eked out a meager existence on poor vegetables and pig fat, to offer themselves the luxury of a nice plump chicken in the pot.

Serves 6
Preparation: 30 minutes
Cooking: 2½ hours
Degree of difficulty:

1 chicken, about 3 lb. (1.5 kg), cleaned out, with its giblets reserved

For the stuffing:
2 oz. (50 g) day-old peasant bread
¾ cup (200 ml) whole milk
1 small onion, finely chopped
1 small garlic clove, finely chopped
2 fresh parsley sprigs, finely chopped
7 oz. (200 g) Bayonne (or Parma) ham, finely chopped
1 egg

For the stock:
1 knuckle of veal (or pork) weighing about 13 oz. (400 g)
8 carrots, halved
4 small turnips, halved
2 leeks, washed and halved
1 small celery stalk, halved
1 onion, with 3 cloves stuck into it
1 garlic clove, unpeeled
Salt and freshly ground black pepper

First prepare your stuffing. Put the bread into a bowl, add the milk, and leave it to soak in. Drain off and discard any excess milk.

Put the onion, garlic, parsley, and ham in a bowl. Finely chop the chicken liver (from the reserved giblets) and add to the bowl with the soaked bread. Mix well.

Break the egg into the mixture, season with salt and pepper, and mix together gently but thoroughly.

Season the inside of the chicken with salt and fill it with the stuffing mixture. Sew up the opening of the chicken with ovenproof thread.

For the stock, fill a large saucepan with cold water. Add the knuckle of veal and remaining chicken giblets. Bring to a boil, skim, then season with salt and pepper. Add the stuffed chicken, bring back to a boil, then reduce the heat, cover, and simmer for 1½ hours.

Add the carrots, turnips, leeks, and celery to the pan, together with the clove-studded onion and garlic. Cover and cook over very gentle heat for another hour, or until the chicken is cooked and tender – it is essential that your chicken does not boil at this stage! Discard the giblets, if preferred.

Check and adjust the seasoning, if necessary. Serve the chicken on a large dish, surrounded by the knuckle of veal, the vegetables, and the stuffing.

King Henry IV's chicken in the pot

Chicken with verbena

Auvergne

Chicken with verbena

This recipe is an acknowledgment to our friend Régis Marcon
who cooks an extraordinary chicken, flavored with verbena,
in a casserole hermetically sealed with flour and water paste, and
serves it in his restaurant along with many other marvelous dishes.
Here, the chicken is simply steamed.
You can serve it with a verbena butter or a sauce made with crème
fraîche and flavored with verbena, or just on its own.

Serves 4 to 6
Preparation: 15 minutes
Cooking: 1½ hours

Degree of difficulty:

1 small brioche made with butter
½ cup (100 ml) milk
½ cup (125 g) ricotta or cottage
  cheese
2 tbsp. (1 oz.) fresh verbena
  (or lemon verbena) leaves
1 small oven-ready chicken,
  about 2½ lb. (1.25 kg)
4 cups (1 l) water
Salt and freshly ground
  black pepper

Prepare the stuffing. Crumble the brioche into a bowl, then
pour the milk over it. Drain off the excess milk, then mix in the
ricotta or cottage cheese. Season with salt and pepper, then add
4 to 5 verbena leaves.

Lightly season the inside of the chicken, spoon the stuffing
into the chicken, and secure the end with ovenproof thread.

Line the bottom of the top section of a steamer with half
the remaining verbena leaves. Put the chicken on top and scatter
the rest of the verbena leaves over the chicken, slipping a few
leaves under the legs and wings.

Pour the measured water into the base of the steamer and bring
to a boil. Place the upper section of the steamer on top of the
base, make sure the chicken is nicely in position, then cover.
Reduce the heat and allow the chicken to simmer gently about
1¼ hours, or until the chicken is cooked and tender. Partially
remove the lid from your steamer for the last 5 minutes of the
cooking time.

Remove the verbena leaves and serve the chicken with cooked
quinoa or steamed zucchini.

Chicken loaf with red wine and coriander

A loaf with very refined flavors! You can make it in advance and eat it cold or gently reheated in the oven. But it's at its best served lukewarm!

Serves 4 to 6
Preparation: 25 minutes, plus marinating
Cooking: 40 minutes
Degree of difficulty:

7 oz. (200 g) cooked skinless boneless chicken breast, diced
2 tbsp. chopped fresh parsley
2 tbsp. chopped fresh coriander
2 onions, thinly sliced
1 garlic clove, chopped
½ cup (100 ml) red wine
½ cup (100 ml) olive oil
1¼ cups (175 g) all-purpose flour
½ packet fast-action dried yeast
2 tbsp. curry powder
1 tsp. salt
3 eggs
½ cup (75 g) ricotta cheese
1 tbsp. grated fresh coconut
Freshly ground black pepper

Prepare the marinade the day before. Put the chicken in a large bowl and cover it with the parsley, coriander, onion, and garlic. Cover this with the red wine and olive oil. Stir to mix, then cover with plastic wrap and put in a cool place or the refrigrator overnight.

Lightly grease an 11 x 4 x 3 in. (28 x 10 x 7 cm) loaf pan and set aside. In a shallow bowl, mix together the flour, yeast, curry powder, and salt, then add some black pepper.

In a separate bowl, mix together the eggs and ricotta cheese, then incorporate them into the flour mixture, mixing well. Finally, add the diced chicken together with the juices from the marinade and mix everything together thoroughly.

Transfer the mixture to the prepared loaf pan and level the surface. Sprinkle the grated coconut over the top. Place in a preheated 350°F (180°C) oven for about 40 minutes or until golden brown and cooked.

Remove from the oven and leave to stand for a few minutes before turning out. Serve warm or cold in slices.

Chicken loaf with red wine
and coriander

Ile-de-France

Corn-fed chicken with red wine

This recipe is a delicious variation on the classic coq au vin. You need a full-bodied red wine that you can then serve at the table to accompany this dish. Here the cock loses one of his last privileges! Serves him right too!

Serves 2 to 4
Preparation: 25 minutes, plus marinating
Cooking: 2½ hours
Degree of difficulty:
1 oven-ready corn-fed chicken, about
  3 lb. (1.5 kg), cut up
8 oz. (250 g) slab bacon, diced
2 tbsp. sunflower oil
8 oz. (250 g) mushrooms, halved
3 tbsp. cognac
2 cups (500 ml) chicken stock
3 tbsp. (25 g) all-purpose flour
¼ stick (25 g) butter
Salt and freshly ground black pepper

For the marinade:
3 cups (750 ml bottle) Burgundy red wine
4 garlic cloves, peeled
10 black peppercorns
10 coriander seeds
1 carrot, chopped
1 fresh thyme sprig
1 fresh parsley sprig
1 bay leaf
Fresh herb sprigs, to garnish

Prepare the marinade the day before. Place the chicken pieces in a large deep dish. Pour over the wine, then add the garlic cloves, peppercorns, coriander seeds, carrot, thyme and parsley sprigs, and bay leaf. Turn to coat the chicken all over with the marinade, then cover and leave in a cool place or the refrigerator overnight. Make sure you turn the chicken pieces from time to time so that they become totally infused with the marinade.

The following day, strain the marinade liquor and put it to one side. Carefully wipe the chicken pieces and reserve them too.

Heat a pan of water to a boil. Add the bacon, then as soon as it returns to a boil, drain and set aside.

Heat 1 tbsp. oil in a high-sided frying pan, add the bacon, and fry over high heat until browned all over. Remove the bacon with a slotted spoon, place it on a plate, and set aside. In the same pan, lightly fry the mushrooms for a few minutes, then season them with salt and pepper and set aside.

Heat the remaining oil in the same pan, add the chicken pieces, and cook over high heat until browned all over, making sure that they are well seared on all sides. Flambé them with the cognac, then put them into a wide heavy bottomed pot together with the bacon and mushrooms.

In a saucepan, bring the strained marinade to a boil and cook about 5 minutes. Pour the hot marinade into the pot, then add enough of the chicken stock to just cover the chicken.

Bring gently to a boil, then reduce the heat, cover, and cook over very gentle heat for about 1¾ hours or until the chicken is cooked and tender. Remove the chicken, bacon, and mushrooms from the pan and keep warm.

Boil the stock in the pan, uncovered, over high heat so that it reduces in volume by half.

Mix the flour and butter in a bowl with 1 tbsp. of the reduced stock. Gradually add this mixture to the hot stock, stirring continuously, and heating until the sauce becomes smooth, thick, and creamy.

Serve the chicken with the mushrooms and bacon topped with the sauce. Garnish with fresh herb sprigs.

Corn-fed chicken with red wine

To be or not to be a good layer?

To be or not to be a good layer? Don't worry, the question is unnecessary – it's easy to recognize the good layers. Firstly, they begin laying around the age of five or six months. Nothing to be proud of! Secondly, they lay for a run of at least two days before reluctantly taking a rest on the third day, just time enough to get their breath. Some go on for three, four, even five days without stopping. In the cause of laying, these tireless workers do the profession a terrible disservice. At that rate, they'll end up making the whole henhouse unemployed!

And lastly, they keep up a maddening regularity, laying every day at the same time! As our Taoist hen would say: "Whether you lay a lot or you lay a little, the farmer will eat you all the same!"

Leghorn

identity tag

Originally from Italy, from where it derives its other name of "Livorno chicken." It emigrated first to the United States, then went on to England around 1875 before coming to rest in France.

cock: 4 to 5¾ lb. (2 to 2.7 kg)
hen: 3½ to 4¾ lb. (1.8 to 2.4 kg)
egg: 2 oz. (55 g), white
varieties: black, white, golden, silver...

United States

Honey loaf with chicken and cumin

A word of advice for cooking this loaf so that it doesn't dry out: Place the loaf pan on a baking sheet rather than directly on the oven shelf. The soft wheat flour gives a delicious nutty flavor to this recipe.

Serves 6
Preparation: 20 minutes, plus marinating
Cooking: 1 hour

Degree of difficulty:

3 tbsp. soy sauce
1 tbsp. honey
1 garlic clove, chopped
5 oz. (150 g) skinless boneless chicken breast,
  cut into small cubes
1⅓ cups (200 g) wheat flour
  (or plain unprocessed flour)
4 tbsp. (50 g) cracked wheat (bulgur)
1 packet active dried yeast
4 eggs, lightly beaten
3 tbsp. olive oil
1 tbsp. dry white wine
2 carrots, grated
5 tbsp. (75 g) cornflakes or wheat flakes
1 tsp. ground cumin
Salt and freshly ground black pepper

Prepare the marinade 2 hours in advance. In a bowl, mix together the soy sauce, honey, and garlic. Add the chicken and stir to mix, then cover with plastic wrap and set aside in a cool place for 2 hours.

Lightly butter an 11 x 4 x 3 in. (28 x 10 x 7 cm) loaf pan and set aside. In a bowl, mix the flour, cracked wheat, and yeast together, then add the eggs, olive oil, and white wine.

Add the chicken pieces and marinade, carrots, cornflakes or wheat flakes, and cumin, season generously with salt and pepper, and mix together well.

Transfer the mixture to the prepared pan and level the surface. Place in a preheated 325°F (160°C) oven for about 1 hour or until golden brown and cooked. Check whether it is cooked by inserting a knife into the loaf: The blade should be almost dry and clean when it comes out. Serve warm or cold in slices.

Honey loaf with chicken and cumin

The hen with the golden eggs

"Avarice, wanting to gain all, loses all.
Only take the case, as legend would recall,
Of the man whose hen, so the story goes,
Every single day a golden egg would lay.
He thought within her body lay treasure nonpareil
So he killed her, opened her, and found her close
In every respect to those whose eggs held no treasure
Yet he himself had destroyed his wealth through his greed, which knew no measure.
For those who are grasping the lesson's not in vain
Since we have lately seen, to many a sigh,
People make themselves poor in the twinkling of an eye
Because they could not wait riches to attain."
La Fontaine

The theme of the hen with the golden eggs, so dear to Aesop and La Fontaine, is to be found throughout the world. Did the hen who invented this subtle ruse think she was going to escape the pot? No chance!

Marans

identity tag

This is the true hen with the golden eggs. Her eggs are a superb russet color, and are magnificent. The Marans comes from a marshy area in the west of France known as the Marais Poitevin, where it is said that passing seafarers cruelly abandoned her!

cock: 7 to 8 lb. (3.5 to 4 kg)
hen: 5¼ to 6½ lb. (2.6 to 3.2 kg)
egg: 2½ oz. (65 g), deep russet red
varieties: silver, golden, white, black speckled, black...

Lemon cream

Proust can keep his madeleine! Here is our version.

Serves 6
Preparation: 15 minutes/Cooking: 30 to 45 minutes
Degree of difficulty:

4 cups (1 l) whole milk
⅔ cup (125 g) superfine sugar
1 tsp. vanilla extract
6 eggs
Grated zest of 1 lemon
Pared lemon zest, to decorate

Lightly butter a shallow 10½ in. (26 cm) baking dish
and set aside. Pour the milk into a large saucepan and heat
for a few moments. Meanwhile, put the sugar, vanilla extract,
and eggs in a bowl and whisk together well.

Slowly pour the hot milk over the egg mixture, whisking
continuously. Stir in the grated lemon zest.

Pour into the prepared dish. Place in a preheated 300°F
(150°C) oven for 30 to 45 minutes or until lightly set.
Serve warm or cold, decorated with pared lemon zest.

You can also cook this recipe in a water bath.

Poitou-Charentes

Eggs *en cocotte* with mixed herbs

Why eggs *en cocotte*? Because, in the old days,
people used to cook them in tiny *"cocottes"* or
cooking pots!
Ultra-simple to prepare, impossible to get wrong,
they are quite delicious as long as you choose really
fresh eggs!

Serves 4
Preparation: 10 minutes/Cooking: 8 to 10 minutes
Degree of difficulty:

8 tsp. thick crème fraîche
8 really fresh eggs
2 tbsp. chopped fresh mixed herbs
Salt and freshly ground black pepper
Chopped fresh chives, to garnish

Lightly butter 8 ramekins or *"cocottes."* Put a teaspoon of
crème fraîche into each ramekin.

Break one egg into each ramekin. Add a little salt and sprinkle
with a pinch of chopped mixed herbs.

Prepare your water bath: Line the bottom of a large, tall-sided
baking pan with a sheet of parchment paper. Place the
ramekins in the pan, then pour in enough boiling water to
come halfway up the sides of the ramekins.

Place in a preheated 325°F (160°C) oven for 8 to 10 minutes or
until just cooked to your liking. Be careful not to overcook the
eggs though! Keep an eye on how they are doing: The white
should be set and the yolk creamy.

Grind a little black pepper over them, garnish with a pinch
of chopped chives, and serve immediately.

Eggs *en cocotte* with mixed herbs

Petits pots de crème (made with eggs and rosewater)

Rosewater goes wonderfully well with eggs. You can flavor an omelet, a mousse, or an egg custard. It is important to cook this recipe using the water-bath method.

Serves 6
Preparation: 20 minutes,
 plus cooling and chilling
Cooking: 20 to 30 minutes

Degree of difficulty:

2 cups (500 ml) whole milk
5 egg yolks
½ cup superfine sugar
1 tbsp. rosewater

Pour the milk into a saucepan, bring it gently to a boil, then remove the pan from the heat and set aside until the milk is lukewarm.

In a bowl, whisk the egg yolks and sugar together until the mixture becomes pale. Pour over the milk, whisking continuously, then stir in the rosewater. Fill 6 small porcelain pots or ramekins with the egg mixture.

Prepare your water bath: Line the bottom of a large, tall-sided baking pan with parchment paper. Arrange the little pots in it, then pour in enough boiling water to come halfway up the sides of the dishes.

Place in a preheated 300°F (150°C) oven about 20 to 30 minutes or until lightly set. They must be cooked slowly so that the cream sets gently. Remove the pots from the oven and let them cool to room temperature.

Store them in the refrigerator and serve very cold.

Petits pots de crème
(made with eggs and rosewater)

The curse of black hens!

The black hen is the outcast of the henhouse, suspected of being in league with the devil. It has long been known that a house with numerous black hens and chicks must belong to sorcerers. That is why, in the old days, they were mercilessly sacrificed at night, at a crossroads! As much to chase away the devil as to make him appear, in the hope that he would reveal where treasure was hidden.

This poor hen was so disliked that they had to change the color of the famous Bresse chickens, who were originally black! The black hen also has the power to find lost money – which might explain our interest in her!

Merlerault

identity tag

From the name of the village in Normandy where she was created. The Merlerault is a sub-species of the Crèvecoeur.

cock: 6 lb. (3 kg)
hen: 5 to 6 lb.
(2.5 to 3 kg)
egg: 2 oz. (55 g), white
variety: black

Ravioli in chicken broth

Ravioli in chicken broth

Ravioli from the Savoie region are made with little balls of spinach (or the green leaves of Swiss chard), which are then combined with cheese and eggs. Here is a variation made with chicken breasts.

Serves 4 to 6
Preparation: 45 minutes, plus resting/Cooking: 15 minutes
Degree of difficulty:

For the pasta:
1⅔ cups (250 g) semolina flour
2 eggs, beaten
about ½ cup (125 ml) lukewarm water

For the stuffing:
2 tbsp. (20 g) butter
2 shallots, chopped
2 tbsp. chopped fresh parsley
7 oz. (200 g) cooked skinless boneless chicken breast,
  cut into thin strips
¾ cup (200 ml) crème fraîche
4 cups (1 l) chicken stock
A few pinches of chopped fresh chives
3 tbsp. (40 g) fresh Parmesan cheese shavings
Salt and freshly ground black pepper

Begin by preparing the pasta. Put the flour into a large bowl, make a well in the center, and pour in the eggs. Add a pinch of salt, then pour in just enough of the measured water, mixing to make a soft dough. Knead gently until smooth and elastic, then cover and leave to rest about 2 hours.

Make the ravioli filling. Gently melt the butter in a frying pan, then add the shallots and parsley and sauté for a few minutes until lightly browned. Remove the pan from the heat and stir in the chicken and crème fraîche. Season with salt and pepper, according to taste.

Roll out the pasta dough into two strips, each about 2½ in. (6 cm) wide. In the center of the first strip of dough, place balls of chicken stuffing measuring about ¾ in. (1.5 cm), leaving a space of about 1½ in. (3.5 cm) between each one. Cover with the second strip of dough. Pinch the outer edges of the dough together and press down firmly with your fingers between each piece of ravioli.

Cut out the ravioli with a pastry wheel, then pinch and close them.

Heat the chicken stock in a large saucepan and add the ravioli as soon as the stock comes to a boil. Reduce the heat a little and cook until they rise to the surface. Remove the ravioli using a slotted spoon and place them in serving bowls.

Pour the chicken broth over the ravioli, add a pinch of chopped chives and a few Parmesan cheese shavings, and serve immediately.

Chicken stew with cognac and orange

Stew as cooked in Provence is a delicious example of a dish gently cooked in a casserole. Traditionally, it is made with beef, but chicken proves to be an excellent alternative in this dish.

Serves 4 to 6
Preparation: 25 minutes, plus marinating/Cooking: 2¾ hours
Degree of difficulty:

Pared zest of 1 orange
1 oven-ready chicken, about 3 lb. (1.5 kg), cut up
2 tbsp. olive oil
8 oz. (250 g) slab bacon, cut into strips
4 onions, thinly sliced
2 ripe tomatoes, skinned and chopped
About 20 mixed black and green olives
Salt and freshly ground black pepper

For the marinade:
2 tbsp. olive oil
5 cups (1.2 l) dry white wine
⅔ cup (150 ml) cognac
10 coriander seeds
10 black peppercorns
1 bouquet garni
4 garlic cloves, (1 crushed and 3 left whole)

The day before, cut the pared orange zest into thin strips and leave them in a warm place to dry out overnight.

Prepare the marinade. Place the chicken pieces in a large, shallow dish and pour over the oil, wine, and cognac. Add the coriander seeds, peppercorns, bouquet garni, and crushed and whole garlic and stir to coat the chicken all over. Cover and leave in a cool place or the refrigerator overnight, stirring from time to time.

The following day, strain the liquor from the marinade and set it aside. Drain the chicken pieces, dry them, and reserve.

Heat 1 tbsp. oil in a large frying pan, add the bacon, and fry over a fairly high heat until browned all over. Remove the bacon from the pan and set aside.

Heat the remaining oil in the same pan, add the onions, and cook until they become transparent, stirring occasionally. Remove the onions from the pan and set aside. Add the chicken pieces to the pan and cook over a high heat until browned all over, turning frequently.

Put the onions and chicken pieces in a baking pan, then pour over the strained marinade. Season, add the orange zest, and bring to the boil. Reduce the heat, cover, and simmer gently for 1 hour.

Transfer the pan to a preheated 300°F (150°C) oven and cook for another hour. Stir in tomatoes, bacon, and olives. Cook for 30 more minutes, or until the chicken is cooked and tender.

Let the stew cool down and serve it a little later, after it has been gently, but thoroughly reheated.

Chicken stewed with
cognac and orange

Counting songs, riddles, and nursery rhymes!

"Humpty Dumpty sat on a wall,
Humpty Dumpty had a great fall;
Three score men and three score more
Cannot place Humpty Dumpty as he was before."
Halliwell, Nursery Rhymes

"A hen on a wall
Pecks away at hard bread
With a shake of her tail
She goes off well fed..."

"When three hens set out for the fields
The first goes in front
The second follows the first
The third comes last
When three hens set out for the fields
The first goes in front..."

The hen is the most familiar creature in counting songs, riddles, and nursery rhymes. All over the world, children learn to read, sing, and count thanks to her.

By the way: Do you know why the Mesopotamian chicken doesn't lay any eggs? And why the Chinese chicken no longer has slanting eyes?

Orpington

identity tag

This lovely English hen was introduced into France around 1900. A good, honest bird, she is very docile and poultry breeders all agree on her qualities.

cock: 7 to 8 lb.
(3.5 to 4 kg)
hen: 5¾ to 7 lb.
(2.8 to 3.5 kg)
egg: 2 to 2½ oz.
(55 to 60 g), yellow
varieties: tawny, black,
white, blue, tricolor,
mottled...

Scotland

Cock-a-leekie

This recipe is dedicated to our friend Susan Smyth whose Scottish grandfather was a cock-a-leekie expert (not to be confused with cock-a-leeko!)

This traditional dish is usually made with a cock, but having tried it with a hen, we can assure you that it is perfectly successful. A chicken broth made with barley and leeks, it is a truly healthy meal!

Serves 4 to 6
Preparation: 25 minutes
Cooking: 2¼ hours
Degree of difficulty:

1 oven-ready hen (or a cock or large chicken), about 3½ lb. (1.75 kg)
⅓ cup (75 g) pearl barley
2 tbsp. sunflower oil
1 onion, chopped
6 leeks, washed and sliced
2 tbsp. chopped fresh parsley
Salt and freshly ground black pepper

Put the chicken into a large cooking pot or saucepan and cover with cold water. Bring to a boil, skim, add a little salt, then cover and leave it to cook gently for about 2 hours, or until the chicken is cooked and tender. Add the pearl barley to the pot about 45 to 60 minutes before the end of the cooking time; the meat should come apart very easily when it is cooked.

As soon as the bird is cooked, remove it from the pot. Strain the stock and set aside, and reserve the pearl barley. Remove and discard the skin from the bird and cut the meat into strips. Keep warm.

Heat the oil in a non-stick frying pan, add the onion, and sauté until lightly browned all over. Add the leeks and sauté until lightly browned. Season to taste with a little black pepper.

Put the strips of chicken, the onion, leeks, and pearl barley into the pot. Pour in the stock and let it simmer for a few minutes over a gentle heat until hot. Adjust the seasoning to taste, if necessary.

Serve the cock-a-leekie very hot in bowls, sprinkled with a little chopped parsley.

Cock-a-leekie

Save the hardy breeds!

Since the end of the 19th century, many breeds of hens have been created by poultry farmers. Most are miniature or ornamental hens. But that doesn't mean that our farmyards are being replenished, because at the same time hardy breeds are declining. Why? Only a very limited number of breeds are reared nowadays, and they are chosen according to criteria linked to the needs of agribusiness which favors "profitable" breeds – the ones which lay more and who don't suffer too much from being confined, from having chemicals administered and being fed with granules. Have you ever visited a battery farm?

Many old breeds, who don't take well to this life of confinement, are thus threatened with extinction. Most farm animals, like draught horses, donkeys, goats, and sheep, are experiencing the same phenomenon.

It has been said, "Man must be persuaded that he does not have the moral right to drive an animal species to extinction" (Jean Dorst).

So, let's fight to save the hardy breeds!

Wyandotte

identity tag

Hardy hen of American origin.

cock: 6½ to 7¾ lb. (3.2 to 3.9 kg)
hen: 5 to 6 lb. (2.5 to 3 kg)
egg: 2 oz. (55 g), from brown to russet
varieties: golden, partridge, cuckoo, blue and black…

Chicken breasts with orange,
grapefruit, and avocado

Chicken and dumplings

Louisiana

Chicken breasts with orange, grapefruit, and avocado

A sweet and sour salad from Louisiana in which the mixture of fruit, soft white cheese, and chutney is very common. Ideal if you want to use up some left-over chicken.

Serves 4
Preparation: 20 minutes
Degree of difficulty:

5 tbsp. soft white cheese,
  such as cream cheese or mascarpone
2 tbsp. mango chutney
1 tsp. curry powder
1 tbsp. honey
1 orange
1 grapefruit
2 avocados
Juice of 1 lemon
2 cooked skinless boneless chicken breasts,
  about 4 oz. (125 g) each, cut into thin strips
Salt and freshly ground black pepper

Prepare the sauce. In a bowl, mix together the soft white cheese, chutney, curry powder, and honey. Season to taste with salt and pepper. Set aside.

Peel the orange and grapefruit. Remove and discard the white pith and cut the fruits into quarters. Set aside.

Peel the avocados, remove and discard the stones, and cut the flesh into small cubes. Sprinkle with a little lemon juice and toss lightly to mix.

Arrange the orange and grapefruit quarters in a large bowl, add the diced avocado and chicken strips, then drizzle over the cheese sauce and serve immediately.

United States

Chicken and dumplings

This was the "Sunday dinner" of the American pioneers. It's a simple and tasty recipe of which there are many variations in different parts of the country.
This is one from Kansas, which we owe to our friends Romig and Lissa Streeter.

Serves 4 to 6
Preparation: 25 minutes/Cooking: 2½ hours
Degree of difficulty:

1 oven-ready chicken, about 3 lb. (1.5 kg), cut up
1 celery stalk, chopped
3 carrots, thinly sliced
2 onions, thinly sliced
1 bay leaf
1 fresh thyme sprig
6 cups (1.5 l) chicken stock

For the dumplings:
2⅓ cups (350 g) all-purpose flour
½ packet active dried yeast
½ tsp. salt
¼ stick (20 g) butter, diced
2 tbsp. chopped fresh dill
1 egg
⅔ cup (150 ml) milk
Salt and freshly ground black pepper
Fresh dill sprigs, to garnish

Put the chicken pieces in a heavy bottomed pot or large saucepan, add the celery, carrots, onions, bay leaf, and thyme. Pour over the chicken stock to cover, adding more water if necessary.

Bring to the boil, add salt and pepper, then reduce the heat, cover and simmer gently for about 2 hours or until the chicken is cooked and tender. Wait until the chicken is perfectly cooked to make the dumplings.

Remove the chicken from the stock, cut it into pieces and then into strips. Set aside and keep warm. Strain the stock, return it to the pan, and reheat it gently until simmering.

Meanwhile, prepare the dumplings. Carefully mix the flour and yeast together in a bowl. Add the salt, butter, and chopped dill. Lightly rub the butter into the flour mixture.

In a second bowl, mix the egg and milk together, then quickly incorporate this into the flour mixture, mixing until smooth.

Using two spoons, form the mixture into little balls about the size of a walnut, then plunge them into the simmering stock.

Cook, uncovered, for 10 minutes, then put the lid on and cook for another 10 minutes.

Drain well and arrange the dumplings on a dish. Serve them accompanied by the sliced chicken and a dish of cooked peas. Garnish with dill sprigs.

The broody ones

The man who sat on eggs

In the old days, if a peasant woman didn't have any good broody hens in her henhouse, she put the eggs in the kitchen near the oven. She might also put them in a basket and cover them with a feather pillow. The warmth did the rest.

But the most effective way of getting the eggs hatched, when there was no devoted hen, was to... call in her husband.

A superb but cruel story by the writer Maupassant – *Toine* – tells how the wife of an innkeeper, who had been paralyzed after a heart attack, forced her husband to stay in bed and hatch some eggs. She refused to feed such a good-for-nothing any longer.

"Toine was defeated. He was forced to sit on the eggs, give up his games of dominoes, and give up any form of movement, for the old woman mercilessly deprived him of food whenever he broke an egg. He laid on his back, looking up at the ceiling, unmoving, his arms raised up like wings, warming the embryos enclosed in their white shells against his body. He spoke only in a whisper now, as if he feared noise as much as movement, and he worried about the yellow hen in her henhouse, engaged in the same task as he was.

He would ask his wife:
'The yellow hen, has she eaten today?'
And the old woman would go from her hens to her husband and from her husband to her hens, obsessed, possessed by the anxiety of the little chickens maturing in the nest and in the bed.
[...]Now, one morning, the wife entered in quite a state and declared:
'The yellow hen has got seven eggs. There were three bad ones.'
Toine could feel his heart beating. How many eggs would *he* have?"

Ardennes

identity tag

Franco-Belgian hen
born in 1913, whose
origin is more Belgian
than French. The
bantam version is
shown here.

cock: 1 lb. 5 oz. (650 g)
hen: 1 lb. 2 oz. (550 g)
egg: 1½ oz. (38 g),
white
varieties: black, white

Are hens stupid?

"The hen has a very low I.Q. You could, without exaggeration, say that she was stupid, but she's good with rice.

The hen has right of reply:

'Perhaps I am stupid, but I'm the one who produces the chicks and has all the bother and worry. I can't rely on the father: he spends his time pecking away in the pub.'

The cock's reply:

'She was the one who wanted chicks, so she can't complain now! It's a hard life, I can tell you.'"

Jean-Louis Fournier

Peking bantam

identity tag

One of the extremely rare breeds of hen, which only exists in bantam form. She was brought back from China in the nineteenth century by the Franco-British expeditionary force, who discovered this little marvel in the emperor's palace.

cock: 1½ lb. to 1 lb. 11 oz. (750 to 850 g)
hen: 1 lb. 7 oz. to 1 lb. 11 oz. (700 to 800 g)
egg: 1¼ oz. (35 g), brown
varieties: black, tawny, blue...

The man who thought he was a cockerel

Once upon a time there was a rich merchant from the city of Bremen. The man had a son, who was the pride and joy of his life, a sweet recompense at the end of his days. The old man imagined the day, not far off now, when his son would succeed him.

But one day, the son woke up and uttered a resounding cock-a-doodle-doo! All day long, he continued his cock-a-doodle-doos. He did the same the next day, and the next, and every day that followed.

In the city of Bremen, they talked of nothing else but the merchant's son who had gone mad and thought he was a cockerel. In vain, the father consulted the most eminent doctors. In vain, he promised to shower with gold anybody who could cure his son of this crazy illness. Nothing worked. Despite all treatments, powders, and ointments, the son continued to utter his heart-rending cock-a-doodle-doos. They were forced to decide he should be shut away.

Then one day a beggar arrived at the rich merchant's door. He claimed to know how to cure his son. The man asked to be left alone with the patient for a few days. When he entered the room, the visitor uttered a joyful cock-a-doodle-doo!

"What! You're a cockerel, too!" exclaimed the sick boy.
"Cock-a-doodle-doo!" replied the visitor.

And there they were, both cock-a-doodle-dooing in unison.
This story took place just before the feast of Yom Kippur.

"I'm worried," said the visitor one morning. "Yom Kippur is approaching and if we continue in this way, we're going to be eaten. So, we shall stop cock-a-doodle-dooing for one week, then, once Yom Kippur is over, we shall sing normally again."

When the father learned that his son was finally cured, he was so overcome with emotion that tears came into his eyes. Of course, he was sad to see that his son could not yet speak. But at least he didn't think he was a cockerel any more: That was the most important thing.

The visitor explained to the rich merchant that his son had promised not to speak for at least a week so that he could ask forgiveness of God and his family. The merchant was moved.

"And you will see," added the visitor, "in a week's time he will be speaking like he did before."

At the synagogue, the boy didn't utter a single cry. After the ceremony, the healer asked for his reward. The merchant handed over a purse filled with gold and even added a horse, richly harnessed, to show his gratitude. The man left the city.

The following day the whole city was awakened by resounding cock-a-doodle-doos.

"It's the rich merchant's son," said the people, "there's the cock-a-doodle-doo coming back to him again!"

After a traditional Jewish story

Barbu d'Anvers

identity tag

Of Belgian origin, this breed was created around 1890. A bantam hen in the featherweight category, she is one of the most popular breeds in Belgium.

cock: 1 lb. 5 oz. (650 g)
hen: 1 lb. 2 oz. (550 g)
egg: 1¼ oz. (35 g),
white
variety: quail

Picardy

Cottage pie with cinnamon chicken

The cinnamon brings a fresh and fragrant note to this unusual cottage pie made with chicken. This is ideal for a meal with friends.

Serves 4 to 6
Preparation: 55 minutes
Cooking: 10 to 15 minutes

Degree of difficulty:

1½ lb. (750 g) potatoes
1¼ cups (300 ml) whole milk
1 tbsp. of butter, plus extra for greasing
½ tsp. ground cinnamon
1 tbsp. sunflower oil
2 onions, thinly sliced
1 lb. (500 g) cooked skinless boneless
   chicken breast, cut into small cubes
3½ oz. (100 g) comté (or gruyere)
   cheese, grated
Salt and freshly ground black pepper

Prepare the mashed potatoes: Wash the potatoes and put them into a saucepan of cold water. Add salt and bring to a boil, then boil gently for about 20 minutes or until cooked. Drain the potatoes, cool slightly, then peel them while they are still warm.

Meanwhile, heat the milk in a saucepan until almost boiling, then remove the pan from the heat and set aside.

Mash the potatoes thoroughly, add the tbsp. of butter and the cinnamon, then gradually pour in the hot milk. Mix well and season with black pepper. Set aside.

Heat the oil in a nonstick frying pan, add the onions, and sauté until they become transparent. Season with black pepper.

Lightly butter a baking dish and put half the mashed potatoes in the bottom of the dish. Cover with a layer of onions, put the diced chicken on top, then spread the remaining mashed potatoes over the top, covering the chicken completely. Sprinkle the cheese over the mashed potatoes and grind some black pepper over the top. Place in a preheated 425°F (220°C) oven for about 10 to 15 minutes, or until the chicken is hot and the potato topping is golden brown.

Serve as soon as it comes out of the oven.

Cottage pie with cinnamon chicken

Chicken in a crust –
a beggar's paradise!

Chicken lends itself to all sorts of methods of cooking: poaching, braising, roasting, steaming...but also to cooking in a flavored crust. Some chefs cook it in a bread dough, others in clay as in the Niger, and still others cook it in a mixture of ash and clay as recommended by the French writer, Colette. She recognized, albeit admiringly, that it was "a rather coarse and primitive delicacy."

The Chinese have an even more tempting recipe: the beggar's recipe. According to a wonderful legend, a beggar stole a hen one day. He hurried away from the scene of the theft, lit a fire, and was getting ready to cook the bird when he heard some noises. Fearing he would be recognized and arrested, he dug a hole in the ground, covered the hen with clay, and quickly buried it in the embers. Once he was certain he had nothing more to fear, he dug into the ground again and unearthed his hen. It was beautifully cooked! The "beggar's chicken" has been a great specialty of Suzhou in China ever since that day.

Faverolles

identity tag

A Normandy hen, who is named after a small village situated between Dreux and Houdan.

cock: 7 to 8 lb. (3.5 to 4 kg)
hen: 5¾ to 7 lb. (2.8 to 3.5 kg)
egg: 2 oz. (55 g), tinted brown
varieties: light, cuckoo...

Chicken terrine
with fresh herbs

Blanquette of
chicken with tarragon

Ile-de-France
Chicken terrine with fresh herbs

A dish to prepare a few hours ahead, before serving it very chilled. For preference, use gelatin obtained from seaweed such as agar agar.

Serves 4 to 6
Preparation: 25 minutes, plus setting and chilling/
Cooking: 15 to 20 minutes
Degree of difficulty:

4 tbsp. water
1 tbsp. (15 g) powdered gelatin
4 cups (1 l) chicken stock
7 oz. (200 g) shelled fresh peas
2 tbsp. chopped fresh chives
2 tbsp. chopped fresh parsley
1 tbsp. chopped fresh tarragon
3 cooked skinless boneless chicken breasts,
  about 4 oz. (125 g) each, cut into thin strips
Salt and freshly ground black pepper

Lightly oil an 11 × 4 × 3 in. (28 × 10 × 7 cm) loaf pan or terrine mold and set aside. Put the measured water into a small bowl and sprinkle the gelatin over the surface. Leave to soften for about 10 minutes, then place the bowl over a pan of simmering water until the gelatin is dissolved, runny, and clear.

Meanwhile, gently warm the chicken stock in a saucepan. Stir in the dissolved gelatin. Remove the pan from the heat and pour enough gelatin mixture into the prepared terrine mold to cover the base. Put the mold in the refrigerator about 30 minutes, or until the aspic is lightly set.

Meanwhile, cook the peas in a pan of salted, boiling water for 5 to 10 minutes, depending on their size, until tender. Drain well and set aside.

Remove the terrine mold from the refrigerator and put a thin layer of chives, parsley, and tarragon over the aspic. Arrange the chicken strips on top of the herbs, together with a generous sprinkling of black pepper. Mix together the peas and remaining fresh herbs, put them into the mold, then pour in the remaining gelatin stock. Chill the terrine in the refrigerator for 3 to 4 hours or until set.

To turn the terrine out, dip the blade of a blunt knife in hot water, and run it along the sides of the terrine. Turn out onto a long plate and serve in slices.

Touraine
Blanquette of chicken with tarragon

This recipe is inspired by the famous blanquette of veal.

Serves 6
Preparation: 15 minutes/Cooking: 1 hour
Degree of difficulty:

¾ cup (200 ml) dry white wine
6 cups (1.5 l) water
1 onion, with 4 cloves stuck into it
1 small celery stalk, roughly chopped
1 garlic clove, peeled and left whole
1 fresh thyme sprig
1 fresh parsley sprig
1 small oven-ready chicken, about 2½ lb. (1.25 kg), cut up
2 carrots, sliced
6 tbsp. (80 g) butter
¼ cup (40 g) all-purpose flour
4 oz. (125 g) mushrooms, cut in half
1 fresh egg yolk
Juice of 1 lemon
3 tbsp. crème fraîche
1 tbsp. chopped fresh tarragon
Salt and freshly ground black pepper
Fresh tarragon leaves, to garnish

Pour the white wine and measured water into a deep heavy bottomed pot. Add the clove-studded onion, celery, garlic, thyme, parsley, and salt and pepper and bring to a boil. Add the chicken pieces and carrots - the liquid should just cover the chicken. Reduce the heat, cover, and cook over a gentle heat for about 20 minutes, skimming the surface from time to time.

Remove the pan from the heat, strain the stock, and reserve the chicken and stock separately. Discard the vegetables and herbs.

Melt 4 tbsp. (55 g) of the butter in a high-sided frying pan, add the chicken pieces, sprinkle with flour, and cook lightly until the chicken becomes golden, turning occasionally. Gradually stir in 1¼ cups (300 ml) of the reserved stock, bring to a boil, stirring, then reduce the heat, cover, and simmer for about 20 minutes.

Meanwhile, melt the remaining butter in a frying pan, add the mushrooms, and sauté for a few minutes, or until lightly browned. Remove the pan from the heat and add the mushrooms to the chicken pan. Cover and cook for a further 10 minutes, or until the chicken is cooked and tender. Remove the chicken and mushrooms from the pan and keep them warm.

Uncover the pan, increase the heat, and boil until the cooking liquid has reduced in volume by about half.

Meanwhile, in a small bowl, mix the egg yolk with the lemon juice and crème fraîche and, away from the heat, gradually stir this mixture into the reduced stock. Add the chopped tarragon and mix well so that the sauce is completely smooth and creamy. Add salt and pepper, to taste.

Pour the sauce over the chicken and mushrooms to serve. Garnish with tarragon leaves and serve with cooked wild rice.

Conversation between a Confucian hen and a Taoist hen

In the East, hens sometimes have conversations that would make our philosophical birds green with envy. Like this one between a Confucian hen and a Taoist hen.

One day a Confucian hen expressed surprise at the small size of the eggs laid by her neighbor, the Taoist hen.

"How do you expect to earn your living with such small eggs? Look, they're half the size of mine. You won't get much for a dozen of *those*, believe me!"

The Taoist hen, who was busy being wooed by a cockerel, looked at the Confucian hen, then at her giant eggs, and replied:

"If you think, my dear, that for a few pence more I'm going to kill myself squeezing out *those* sort of eggs, you've got another think coming!"

identity tag

A very old Japanese breed, of which traces have been found dating to the 16th century. Also known as the Chabo.

cock: 7 to 8 lb. (3.5 to 4 kg)
hen: 5¾ to 7 lb. (2.8 to 3.5 kg)
egg: 2 to 2½ oz. (55 to 60 g), yellow
varieties: black, white, blue, buff...

Japanese

A real mother hen

"In that place there is an extraordinary phenomenon which is worth recounting. Would you believe, they have hens with no feathers but fur just like cats. They are black, with eggs like ours, and they are excellent to eat."

Marco Polo, *Description of the World*

This admirable little hen, described by Marco Polo, was the Negro-silk. She owes her name to the silky look of her feathers and the black color of her skin. The Negro-silk is rarely eaten nowadays, precisely because of this black color, which is not considered to be very appetizing, and also because of her weight of feathers. It's true that there's not much left to feast on!

That doesn't stop her being the darling of poultry breeders. Although she is a modest layer, she is exceptionally good at incubating her eggs (even in snow) and is a real mother hen who cares wonderfully for her chicks. She doesn't bother too much about where the eggs come from. Chicken eggs, duck eggs, hen pheasant or ceramic eggs, they're all the same! One day she'll end up sitting on her own shadow! What is more, she rears and trains her chicks and watches over them with exemplary devotion. She's a model of patience and endurance and we're left full of admiration!

Negro-silk

identity tag

This Japanese hen was already known in France in the 18th century and was highly regarded by the writer and naturalist, Buffon.

cock: 2 lb. (1 kg)
hen: 1 lb. 10 oz. (800 g)
egg: 1½ oz. (40 g)
varieties: black, blue, silver gray, wild...

Christopher Columbus' egg!

This great navigator had to confront not only unknown territories and uncharted seas. He also had the jealousies and sarcasms of the Spanish court dignitaries to contend with, which was no small task. Here too, he demonstrated much cool-headedness and presence of mind, if we are to believe the following anecdote.

During a reception, one of the nobles, irritated by the sudden fame of the new viceroy to the new countries (that was his title), pointed out that this celebrated voyage to the Indies was not really so difficult.

Upon which Christopher Columbus seized an egg from a table and said:

"You are entirely right, but tell me, would you be able to balance this egg?"

Seeing the noble's confusion – he did not know what to reply to this enigmatic question – Christopher Columbus broke the egg at one end and put it down vertically.

"My voyage to the Indies was like keeping this egg upright. You are quite right, it was simple, but you had to know how to go about it!"

This is what is known as egg-proof!

110

Padovana

identity tag

This hen with her
proud crest was once
an Italian hardy hen.
She was selected in
England.

cock: 2 lb. (1 kg)
hen: 1 lb. 10 oz. (800 g)
egg: 1¼ oz. (35 g)
varieties: black, white,
chamois, golden, blue,
cuckoo...

Risotto with chicken stock
and wild asparagus tips

Risotto with chicken stock and wild asparagus tips

This *riso cotto*, literally meaning "cooked rice," is even better when it's prepared with good, homemade chicken stock.

Serves 4
Preparation: 10 minutes/Cooking: 30 to 35 minutes
Degree of difficulty:

4 tbsp. (50 g) butter
1¼ cups (200 g) Arborio risotto rice
2 cups (500 ml) white wine
4 cups (1 l) chicken stock
2 shallots, chopped
5 oz. (150 g) asparagus tips (wild asparagus tips,
  if you can get them), chopped
2 tbsp. (20 g) fresh Parmesan cheese, grated
1 tbsp. chopped fresh parsley
Salt and freshly ground black pepper

Melt ¼ stick (20 g) of the butter in a heavy bottomed saucepan and add the rice. Cook for a few minutes, then add the white wine. Cook gently, stirring frequently, until all the wine has been absorbed by the rice, then pour in a little stock. Cook gently, until the rice has absorbed all the stock, then again pour in 3 or 4 tbsp. of stock. Gradually add all the remaining stock in this way, stirring frequently, then cover the pan and leave the rice to cook over a very gentle heat, while preparing the asparagus.

Melt the remaining butter in a nonstick frying pan, add the shallots, and sauté for 2 minutes. Add the asparagus tips and sauté gently for 2 to 3 minutes or until tender. Gently fold the shallots and asparagus tips into the risotto. Stir in the Parmesan, then season to taste with salt and pepper. When the risotto has become very smooth and creamy, sprinkle some chopped parsley over the top and serve immediately.

Frittata with chicken and basil

A frittata is an Italian omelet. Unlike in the French tradition, frittata is served well cooked on both sides.

Serves 4
Preparation: 15 minutes/Cooking: 15 minutes
Degree of difficulty:

8 eggs, beaten
1 cooked skinless boneless chicken breast,
  about 4 oz. (125 g), cut into thin strips
2 tbsp. chopped fresh basil leaves
1 small bunch of fresh parsley, chopped
1 tbsp. olive oil
Salt and freshly ground black pepper
Fresh herb sprigs, to garnish

Mix the eggs, chicken, basil and parsley together in a large bowl. Season generously with salt and pepper.

Heat the oil in a nonstick frying pan and pour in the egg mixture.

Cover and cook over a low heat for about 10 minutes.

Slide the frittata onto a flat plate and then return it to the frying pan the other side up. Cook gently for 5 more minutes or until golden brown on both sides.

Cut the frittata into small rectangles or diamond shapes, garnish with fresh herb sprigs, and serve warm.

Chicken rolls with olives and red wine

If you have a little time at your disposal, try this very original recipe. Nothing is nicer than making your own bread.

Serves 6
Preparation: 25 minutes, plus rising/Cooking: 15 to 20 minutes
Degree of difficulty:

1⅓ cups (200 g) white bread flour
1 cup (150 g) whole wheat flour
1 packet (7 g) active dried yeast
1 tsp. salt
1 cup (250 ml) red wine
1 tbsp. olive oil
5 oz. (150 g) skinless boneless chicken breast, finely chopped
3½ oz. (100 g) pitted black olives, finely chopped

Lightly flour a baking sheet and set aside. Put the two flours, yeast, salt, and red wine into the bowl of your electric mixer or food processor, fitted with a dough hook or dough blade.

Knead for 5 minutes on a slow speed, then add the olive oil, chicken, and olives. Increase the speed slightly and knead for a further 5 minutes. (Alternatively, put the flours, yeast, salt, and red wine in a bowl and knead together by hand to form a dough. Turn out onto a lightly floured surface and knead gently for 5 minutes, then knead in the olive oil, chicken, and olives. Knead the dough for another 5 minutes).

Place the dough in a shallow oiled dish, cover with a cloth, and leave to rest at room temperature for 45 minutes. The dough will slowly rise during this time.

Divide the dough into equal portions, then shape the dough into round or long rolls of the same size. Place them on the prepared baking sheet and cover with a cloth. Leave to rest at room temperature for another 45 minutes.

Brush the rolls with a little water, then place in a preheated 400°F (200°C) oven for about 15 to 20 minutes or until cooked, risen, and lightly browned. Transfer the rolls to a wire rack to cool and serve warm or cold.

Mimosa-style bruschetta with tapenade

A simple and tasty way of enjoying hard-boiled eggs!

Serves 4
Preparation: 15 minutes/Cooking: 5 minutes
Degree of difficulty:

4 to 8 slices of peasant bread, depending on size of loaf
  (or crusty French bread)
1 small jar of tapenade, about 6 oz. (175 g)
4 hard-boiled eggs
1 tbsp. chopped fresh chives
Salt and freshly ground black pepper

Place the slices of bread under a preheated broiler and toast until lightly browned on both sides.

Remove them from the grill and let them cool for a few moments, then spread the toast with a layer of tapenade.

Shell the eggs and separate the egg whites from the yolks. Use the egg whites for another recipe. Put the egg yolks into a sieve held above the slices of toast and press the yolks through the sieve with the back of a spoon, to create little yellow vermicelli which will color your bruschetta. Grind some black pepper over the top.

Sprinkle with some chopped chives and serve.

Chicken rolls with olives
and red wine

Go on, brood, broody hen, there will always be plenty of eggs!

A cock can "mate" with a hen several times a day: Is the hen always in agreement with this? We don't know. But the cock's vitality means that there is always a considerable number of fertilized eggs to be hatched.

To hatch, these eggs must be incubated for the 10 days after laying takes place. The ones who are good at sitting on their eggs and brooding, those who know how to "run the nest," will keep their eggs warm for 21 days. For the chicks in a hurry to get out, 20 days will be enough! Hens turn the eggs over with their feet from time to time in order to spread the heat better.

The temperature of the eggs must remain at around 100°F (38.5°C). A sudden fever that brings them up to 104°F (40°C), and the chicks are done for!

We will not mention the artificial incubators, which can store and incubate nearly 15,000 eggs at the same time. A good broody hen would never find her eggs!

Rhode Island

identity tag

Created around 1860 in the State of Rhode Island (United States), this hardy hen is very highly regarded by breeders.

cock: 6 lb. 10 oz. to 8 lb. (3.3 to 4 kg)
hen: 5¼ to 6 lb. (2.6 to 3 kg)
egg: 2½ oz. (60 g), russet
variety: red

Souffle omelet with maple syrup

Maple syrup has a slightly caramelized flavor, and is a very interesting cooking ingredient. It gives a unique flavor to the souffle omelet in this recipe.
This omelet is to be eaten as soon as it comes out of the oven!

Serves 4 to 6
Preparation: 20 minutes/Cooking: 10 minutes
Degree of difficulty:

6 egg whites
Pinch of salt
5 egg yolks
½ cup (100 ml) maple syrup
2 tbsp. rum
2 tbsp. (20 g) butter
1 tbsp. sunflower oil
2 tbsp. brown sugar

Whisk the egg whites in a large bowl until they stand up in stiff peaks. Don't forget to add a pinch of salt, which will make them go stiff even more quickly!

Put the egg yolks, maple syrup, and rum in a separate large bowl and stir together until well mixed. Carefully fold in half the whisked egg whites, mixing gently but thoroughly, and then fold in the remaining whisked egg whites.

Heat the butter and oil in a nonstick, ovenproof frying pan, pour in the egg mixture, and cook over fairly high heat for 2 to 3 minutes. Remove the pan from the heat and place it in a preheated 400°F (200°C) oven for about 3 to 5 minutes, or until the omelet is lightly set and golden brown on top.

Carefully transfer the souffle omelet to a serving plate, sprinkle it with brown sugar, and serve immediately.

Canada

Acadian casserole

This is the "Sunday gratin." In Acadia, this chicken, poached and then put in the oven to form a crust on top, is traditionally served from the casserole it was cooked in, which then goes directly onto the table.

Serves 4 to 6
Preparation: 25 minutes/Cooking: 2½ hours
Degree of difficulty:

1 oven-ready chicken, about 3 lb. (1.5 kg), cut up
6 cups (1.5 l) vegetable stock
5 large potatoes, sliced
2 large onions, chopped
Fresh savory sprigs (or fresh thyme or tarragon sprigs)
Salt and freshly ground black pepper

Place the chicken pieces in a heavy bottomed pot and pour in the vegetable stock – it should just cover the chicken. Bring to a boil, then reduce the heat immediately. Cover and cook over low heat for about 1½ hours.

Carefully remove the chicken from the stock, cool slightly, then remove and discard the skin and bones from the chicken. Break the meat into pieces. Strain and reserve the stock.

Lightly grease a large ovenproof casserole dish. Line the bottom of the prepared dish with a layer of half the potatoes. Season generously with salt and pepper, then cover with half the chicken. Top this with a layer of onions and season, then sprinkle with a few sprigs of savory.

Arrange a second layer of the remaining potatoes over the savory, then top with the remaining chicken. Season and top with a few sprigs of savory.

Pour over the reserved chicken stock, cover and place in a preheated 375°F (190°C) oven for about 1 hour or until the potatoes are tender. Serve.

Soufflé omelet
with maple syrup

Chicken breasts stuffed with wild rice and mushrooms

For this recipe, you can also use boneless chicken breasts with their skin on and stuff them without cutting into the meat, by simply sliding the stuffing under the skin. The meat will be even more tender and flavorsome.

Serves 4 to 6
Preparation: 20 minutes/Cooking: 45 to 55 minutes

Degree of difficulty:

¼ cup (40 g) wild rice
1 tbsp. butter
1 shallot, chopped
3½ oz. (100 g) fresh chanterelle mushrooms (or other fresh
  wild mushrooms such as oyster mushrooms), cleaned
4 skinless boneless chicken breasts, about 4 oz. (125 g) each
1 to 2 tbsp. sunflower oil
Salt and freshly ground black pepper

Cook the wild rice in a pan with 1 cup of salted, boiling water for about 25 to 30 minutes, or until tender. Drain and set aside.

Melt the butter in a frying pan, add the shallot and mushrooms, and sauté for about 3 minutes. Season with salt and pepper, then stir in the cooked rice.

Slit the chicken breasts on one side, season the insides with salt and pepper, then spoon some stuffing into each breast. Close up each chicken breast over the filling and secure with wooden toothpicks.

Heat the oil in a frying pan, add the stuffed chicken breasts, and fry over medium heat about 15 to 20 minutes, or until the chicken is cooked and tender.

For best results, make sure you do not overcook the chicken, or it may dry out. Serve hot.

Chicken and guacamole sandwich

A sandwich in a wink of an eye, Tex-Mex style. If you have a bit more time, you can make the guacamole yourself by mixing the flesh of 2 very ripe avocados with a small chopped onion, the juice of half a lemon and a few drops of Tabasco sauce.

Serves 4
Preparation: 10 minutes

Degree of difficulty:

8 slices of bread
½ cup (125 g) guacamole
12 thin slices of cooked skinless boneless chicken breast
2 tbsp. chopped fresh coriander leaves
Freshly ground black pepper

Spread 4 slices of bread with guacamole. Cover with slices of chicken, grind some black pepper over the top, then sprinkle with chopped coriander. Cover each with a second slice of bread.

Cut each sandwich in half to make 2 triangles and serve immediately.

English customs

The English are passionate about poultry breeding. They have created, selected, and improved countless breeds and are responsible for most of the lovely foreign breeds that have arrived in Europe.

Naturally, this passion gave rise to certain beliefs and customs.

For example, in the old days, newly married couples were given a nice farm hen as a present. A symbol of fertility, the hen was seen to promise happiness, prosperity, and numerous descendants.

Another piece of English country folklore says that if hens perch at midday, it means that the farmer is going to die!

Sussex

identity tag

A hardy English hen, who is capable of standing up to the hardest of winters. She comes from the county of Sussex and is a superb farm hen.

cock: 7 to 8 lb. (3.5 to 4 kg)
hen: 6 to 7 lb. (3 to 3.5 kg)
egg: 2½ oz. (70 g), white tinted
varieties: speckled, tricolor, black, tawny, buff, mottled, gray...

Chicken pie with
mustard seeds

England

Chicken pie with mustard seeds

Don't forget the Worcestershire sauce! That's what gives that special little flavor to some English cooking. It's a mixture of malt vinegar, molasses, and soy sauce, for which the precise recipe has been kept a secret since it was created in the 19th century.

Serves 4
Preparation: 40 minutes
Cooking: 20 to 25 minutes

Degree of difficulty:

5 potatoes, cut into small chunks
1 tbsp. sunflower oil
2 onions, thinly sliced
2 tbsp. all-purpose flour
½ tsp. mustard seeds
1¼ cups (300 ml) chicken stock
1 lb. (500 g) cooked skinless boneless
  chicken breast, cut into thin strips
1 tbsp. Worcestershire sauce
2 tbsp. chopped fresh parsley
1½ tbsp. of butter
6 tbsp. milk
Salt and freshly ground black pepper

Lightly grease a 9 in. (22 cm) gratin or baking dish and set aside. Cook the potatoes in a pan of salted, boiling water for about 20 minutes or until tender. Drain well, keep warm, and set aside.

Meanwhile, heat the oil in a frying pan, add the onions, and sauté until lightly browned. Add a little black pepper, then stir in the flour and mustard seeds and cook gently for 1 minute, stirring. Gradually stir in the stock, then heat gently, stirring, until the sauce comes to the boil and thickens. Simmer gently for a few minutes, stirring.

Add the chicken strips, Worcestershire sauce, and chopped parsley and stir to mix. Remove the pan from the heat and set aside.

Put the cooked potatoes into a large bowl with the butter and milk. Mash them all together until smooth and creamy. Season with salt and pepper.

Spoon the chicken mixture into the prepared dish, then cover it completely with the mashed potatoes.

Place in a preheated 400°F (200°C) oven for 20 to 25 minutes or until the potato topping is golden brown. Serve very hot.

Egg flip flan

This flan is very easy to make but the finished effect is very impressive.

Serves 6
Preparation: 25 minutes, plus chilling
Cooking: 50 minutes to 1 hour 5 minutes

Degree of difficulty:

12 oz. (350 g) pie dough
3 eggs
½ cup (100 g) superfine sugar
1 tbsp. vanilla sugar
  (or 1 to 2 tsp. vanilla extract)
2 tbsp. cornstarch
Finely grated zest of ½ lemon
2 cups (500 ml) whole milk
¾ cup (200 ml) crème fraîche
3 tbsp. rum
Confectioner's sugar, for dusting
Sugar flowers or crystallized flowers,
  to decorate

Lightly butter a 10 in. (25 cm) flan or baking dish and line it with the rolled-out pastry. Prick the pastry all over with a fork. Line the pastry dough with parchment paper, fill with a layer of baking beans, and bake blind in a preheated 400°F (200°C) oven for 15 minutes. Remove the beans and paper and return the pastry crust to the oven for 5 minutes. Remove from the oven and set aside. Reduce the oven temperature to 325°F (160°C).

Meanwhile, prepare the filling. Put the eggs, superfine sugar, and vanilla sugar in a large bowl and whisk together until well mixed. Add the cornstarch and lemon zest and whisk to mix. Add the milk, crème fraîche, and rum, whisking all the time, until well mixed. Pour the egg mixture into the pastry crust.

Bake in the oven for 30 to 45 minutes or until the flan is lightly set and golden brown. Remove from the oven and set aside to cool. Once cool, carefully turn out onto a plate and chill well before serving.

Dust with sifted confectioner's sugar and decorate with sugar flowers or crystallized flowers. Serve in slices.

Egg flip flan

Those who could
care less

Chickens on trial

In the Middle Ages, trials of animals were quite frequent. In the 12th century, judges summoned May bug larvae to appear in court! They were accused of destroying vegetable roots in gardens. As they could not put forward anything in their defense, they were sentenced to exile and had to "withdraw to an uninhabited region."

Fowl did not escape these excesses. In 1374, a cock was burnt alive in a public place with an egg at his side. The judges accused him of having laid it himself!

According to the beliefs of the time, eggs laid by cocks hid snakes, foul beasts, and all manner of diabolical creatures!

Appenzeller

identity tag

Originally from the
Appenzell region,
this is a very
popular hen in
Switzerland.

cock: 3 to 3½ lb.
(1.5 to 1.8 kg)
hen: 2½ to 3 lb.
(1.2 to 1.5 kg)
egg: 2 oz. (55 g),
white
varieties: silver,
golden, blue,
black...

Chicken thieves, chicken eaters!

For a long time, the hen was a very precious commodity in the countryside. It was thanks to hens that generations of peasants and their families were able to survive. That was why "chicken thieves" were very looked down upon. And people showed no mercy in chasing them off.

It was easy to accuse strangers, people passing through, gypsies, actors, and other hawkers and peddlers of being specialists in this kind of plundering. Till Ulenspiegel, the mischievous and humorous hero of the town of Damme, knew something about it!

As for the expression "chicken eaters," it was a way of expressing contempt. Flemish people, for example, called those from Brussels *kiekefretters*, i.e., chicken eaters, because when they won the battle of Sheut in the 15th century, the only valuables they found in the enemy's camp were... hundreds of chickens!

Brakel

identity tag

A very old Belgian hen,
already in existence in
the 14th century.

cock: 4 to 5 lb. 7 oz.
(2 to 2.7 kg)
hen: 3½ to 5 lb.
(1.7 to 2.5 kg)
egg: 2 oz. (55 g), white
varieties: silver, golden,
chamois, white, black...

Belgium

Chicken *waterzoï*

This is a classic of Belgian cuisine. *Waterzoï* is a dish of Flemish origin made with freshwater fish (eel, pike, carp, gudgeon, perch...) or fish from the North Sea (cod, turbot, whiting, sole...). *Waterzoï* can also be made with poultry, and the town of Ghent is most famous for this dish. Here is a version that is very easy to prepare.

Serves 4 to 6
Preparation: 15 minutes
Cooking: 1¼ hours

Degree of difficulty:

½ stick (50 g) butter
2 onions, thinly sliced or finely
  chopped
10 oz. (300 g) carrots, finely chopped
1 celery stalk, thinly sliced
1 small oven-ready chicken,
  about 2½ lb. (1.25 kg), cut up
A handful of fresh parsley sprigs
1 bouquet garni
4 cups (1 l) chicken stock
1 egg yolk
¾ cup (200 ml) crème fraîche
Salt and freshly ground black pepper
Fresh parsley leaves, to garnish

Melt half the butter in a heavy bottomed sauté pan, then add the onions, carrots, and celery and sauté until lightly browned all over. Remove the vegetables to a plate and keep warm.

Melt the remaining butter in the pan, add the chicken pieces, and sauté until lightly browned all over, turning once. Return the vegetables to the pan and add the parsley sprigs and bouquet garni.

Season with salt and pepper, then cover and cook for 10 minutes over low heat. Add the stock, bring to a boil, then reduce the heat, cover, and simmer gently about 35 to 45 minutes or until the chicken is cooked and tender.

Remove and discard the parsley sprigs and bouquet garni and arrange the chicken joints on a serving dish. Keep warm.

Add the egg yolk and crème fraîche to the pan and heat gently, stirring continuously with a wooden spoon, until the sauce thickens.

Spoon the sauce over the chicken, garnish with parsley leaves, and serve with slices of toast.

Chicken waterzoi

Cock fights

Come to that, have you ever heard of hen fights?

Little English fighting cock

identity tag

Cock fighting was forbidden in England in 1849. The English fighting cock was among the most famous of the fighting breeds, but has since been turned into an ornamental bantam hen!

cock: 1 lb. 3 oz. (600 g)
hen: 1 lb. (500 g)
egg: 1 oz. (25 g), light brown
varieties: golden, silver

Indian fighting cock

identity tag

Its origin is a subject of controversy. Perhaps it is a crossbreed between English and Malayan fighting cocks!

cock: 9 to 10 lb. (4.5 to 5 kg)
hen: 8 lb. (4 kg)
egg: 3 oz. (70 g)
varieties: pheasant brown, white, tawny...

Once upon a time there was a bailey!

In the Middle Ages, knights' castles were usually made up of a keep and an initial enclosed courtyard protected by inner walls: This was known as the outer ward.

It was there that the lord and his family resided. It was there too that arms and supplies were stored. In the outer ward, the lord meted out justice and conducted proceedings between those who were under his jurisdiction.

Then there was a second courtyard, more spacious and also surrounded by solid walls. Here there was a church, a blacksmith, a saddler, a well, a fountain, barns, stables, and cowsheds – a real village, in fact, where the peasants took refuge in the event of an attack. In the middle of this courtyard, hens and cockerels, oxen and horses, and all sorts of farm animals frolicked about. This was called the inner ward or bailey, from the old French *"baille"* (enclosed court) – and the *"basse-cour,"* which is the name still given today in French to the place reserved for hens and chickens and small farm animals.

Crèvecoeur

identity tag

A very old French breed which is named after a small village in Normandy.

cock: 6 lb. (3 kg)
hen: 6 lb. (3 kg)
egg: 2 oz. (55 g), white
varieties: black, white, cuckoo, blue...

Normandy

Chicken with cider and calvados

Apples, cream, cider, calvados... there's no doubt we're in Normandy! A celebration dish that is really very simple to make.

Serves 4 to 6
Preparation: 20 minutes
Cooking: 1 to 1¼ hours

Degree of difficulty:

3 *reinette* or empire apples
Pinch of ground cinnamon
1 small oven-ready chicken,
  about 2½ lb. (1.25 kg)
1 cup or 1 bottle (275 ml) of dry
  sparkling cider
¼ cup (50 ml) calvados
4 tbsp. crème fraîche
Salt and freshly ground black
  pepper
Fried apple slices, to serve

Peel and core the apples, then cut them into quarters. Sprinkle the apples with the cinnamon and salt and pepper and put them inside the cavity of the chicken. Put the chicken in a baking pan and season all over with salt and pepper. Pour less than 1 cup (250 ml) of cider into the baking pan.

Place in a preheated 375°F (190°C) oven about 1 to 1¼ hours, or until the chicken is cooked and tender. Turn the chicken once or twice during the cooking time so that it browns on all sides and baste the chicken regularly with the juices.

Remove the chicken from the oven and flambé it quickly with the calvados. Place the chicken on a plate and keep warm.

Deglaze the cooking juices in the pan by adding the remaining cider. Let it bubble and reduce over the heat, then pour in the crème fraîche and stir with a wooden spoon until it thickens.

Pour the sauce over the chicken and serve with fried apple slices.

Chicken with cider and calvados

Chicken weather forecast

"If when it rains the hens run and hide,
The rain will stop; they won't stay inside,
But if they persist in staying out in the wet,
The rain won't stop, on that you can bet."
As this saying suggests, hens are able to predict what the weather is going to be like.
Of course, you have to know how to interpret their movements and actions, which not everybody is capable of doing!
Hens are considered to be more reliable than frogs and, what's more, frogs need a ladder!

Spanish

identity tag

This Spanish hen was selected in England during the reign of King Philip II of Spain.

cock: 6 to 7¼ lb. (3 to 3.6 kg)
hen: 5 to 6 lb. (2.5 to 3 kg)
egg: 2 oz. (55 g), white
variety: black

Chicken with chocolate

When we tasted this Mexican-inspired dish for the first time, we didn't imagine that it would become one of our favorite recipes. The sauce is so delicious that it's best to prepare a bit extra!

Serves 4 to 6
Preparation: 25 minutes, plus soaking/Cooking: 55 minutes
Degree of difficulty:

5 small dried red chilies
2 tbsp. sunflower oil
1 small oven-ready chicken, about 2½ lb. (1.25 kg), cut up
2 onions, finely chopped
2 garlic cloves, finely chopped
5 tomatoes, skinned and finely chopped
¾ cup (75 g) ground almonds
1 tsp. ground cinnamon
1 tsp. ground coriander
½ tsp. freshly ground black pepper
3 tbsp. (40 g) dark bitter chocolate (70% cocoa solids), roughly chopped
¾ cup (200 ml) chicken stock
Salt, to taste
Small whole fresh red chilies, to garnish

Put the dried chilies in a bowl and just cover them with lukewarm water. Leave to soak for 20 minutes.

Heat the oil in a heavy bottomed saucepan, add the chicken pieces, and cook over fairly high heat until browned all over, turning frequently. Remove the chicken pieces to a plate and set aside.

Meanwhile, strain the chilies, reserving the chilies and soaking water separately. Seed and finely chop the chilies, then put the chilies and their soaking water into the bowl of a food processor or blender. Add the onions, garlic, tomatoes, almonds, cinnamon, coriander, and black pepper and puree until smooth and well mixed. (Alternatively, place all these ingredients in a bowl and mix together thoroughly.)

Pour this puree into the saucepan and let it cook gently for 5 minutes. Add the dark chocolate and stir until melted, then stir in the chicken stock.

Return the chicken pieces to the saucepan. Add salt to taste, bring gently to a boil, then reduce the heat, cover, and cook very gently for about 30 minutes, or until the chicken is cooked and tender.

Serve the chicken with the chocolate sauce poured over. Garnish with small fresh chilies and serve with boiled rice.

Chicken with chocolate

Chicken breasts with orange,
chervil, and chives

Spain

Chicken breasts with orange, chervil, and chives

Try this recipe inspired by a dish from the region of Valencia. Chicken and orange make a very felicitous combination.

Serves 4
Preparation: 10 minutes/Cooking: 35 minutes

Degree of difficulty:

1 tbsp. olive oil
4 small skinless boneless chicken breasts,
  about 3½ oz. (100 g) each
Juice of 4 oranges
½ cup (100 ml) dry white wine
⅔ cup (150 ml) chicken stock
1 tbsp. chopped fresh chervil leaves
1 tbsp. chopped fresh chives
Salt and freshly ground black pepper

Heat the oil in a nonstick frying pan over medium heat. Add the chicken breasts and fry until the chicken is cooked and tender and browned on both sides, turning occasionally. Season with salt and pepper, then remove from the pan, place on a plate, and keep warm.

Pour the orange juice, white wine, and chicken stock into the frying pan. Scrape the bottom of the pan so that any bits of meat are well mixed into the sauce. Bring to a boil, then reduce the heat and simmer gently for about 12 minutes. Taste and adjust the seasoning.

Pour the sauce over the chicken breasts and sprinkle with chopped chervil and chives. Grind some black pepper over the top and serve.

Chicken gazpacho Andalusian-style

In the Bible there is a passage referring to "a food that can be drunk." This mysterious recipe, which for a long time puzzled historians and food-lovers alike, is in reality gazpacho, whose Arabic name means "soaked bread." It became a great specialty of Andalusia, and here it is enriched with chicken pieces.

Serves 4 to 6
Preparation: 25 minutes, plus standing and chilling

Degree of difficulty:

3 garlic cloves, peeled
3 slices of peasant bread (or French bread)
5 tbsp. olive oil
1 lb. (500 g) ripe tomatoes, skinned and finely chopped
1 yellow pepper, seeded and finely chopped
1 small cucumber, finely chopped
1 onion, finely chopped
1 cooked skinless boneless chicken breast,
  about 4 oz. (125 g), finely chopped
3 tbsp. sherry vinegar
Salt and freshly ground black pepper

Crush the garlic in a mortar and add a pinch of salt. Crumble the bread over the garlic, then pour over the olive oil, rubbing the mixture with your fingertips until everything is evenly distributed. Leave it to stand for about 30 minutes.

Put the tomatoes, yellow pepper, cucumber, and onion into the bowl of a food processor or blender. Add the chicken, vinegar, soaked bread, and seasoning. Blend everything together until it is very finely chopped. Transfer the gazpacho to a serving bowl and chill it in the refrigerator for at least 2 hours before serving.

Luxury hens

Luxury or ornamental hens have become a great passion with amateur poultry breeders. They all dream of having these hens, with their superb colors and unusual plumage, as a feature of their farm or country residence. Some of the hens recall the canvases of De Kooning, others are reminiscent of the imaginary journeys depicted by Michaux or the paintings of Bazaine. Others still recall Zao Wou-ki.

These ornamental hens are often bantams. What did you expect!

We live in an age when the miniature is highly prized!

Hamburg

identity tag

Formerly a good layer,
she was later turned
into a luxury hen.
Her name comes from
the port of Hamburg
on the North Sea coast.
However, she appears
to have been selected
in England and born in
Asia.

cock: 2 lb. (950 g)
hen: 1 lb. 10 oz. (800 g)
egg: 1¼ oz. (35 g)
varieties: golden,
silver spangled, golden
spangled...

Grandmothers' remedies, sorceresses' secrets!

Long versed in the arts of healing and highly knowledgeable about herbalism, witches reared hens in order to prepare their love potions, poisons, and ointments.

"Take a new-laid egg, place it in an ants' nest without anyone seeing you (an essential condition for success), say the magic words, and you will be cured of your fever."

The hen was also highly valued by exorcists and followers of black magic: Her throat was slit and her blood poured over the bodies of persons possessed, or of postulants.

Popular beliefs and "pieces of advice" concerning life's little ills survived for a very long time, inherited from these ancestral practices. When a child was slightly injured, the wound was rubbed with "chicken urine." To cure chilblains, an egg was beaten up with brandy and the affected place rubbed with it. To stop whitlow, you just needed to dip your finger into a fresh egg which had had the pointed end of its shell broken. After twelve hours, the finger would have healed! As for bronchitis, pneumonia and other chest inflammations, there was no better cure than to smear chicken fat over the patient. And as the hen obviously had a use for everything, you simply gathered her droppings in order to heal burns.

If you wanted your child to talk at an early age, you had to give him or her the first egg laid by a young hen to eat.

By comparison with such resourceful medicine, doctors were often considered to be useless charlatans.

White-crested Dutch hen

identity tag

This breed comes from the Netherlands, where she has been present for more than five centuries. The bantam version was exhibited for the first time in 1917.

cock: 3¾ to 4½ lb. (1.9 to 2.2 kg)
hen: 2¾ to 3¼ lb. (1.4 to 1.6 kg)
egg: 1½ oz. (45 g), white
varieties: black with white crest, cuckoo, blue, white, mottled...

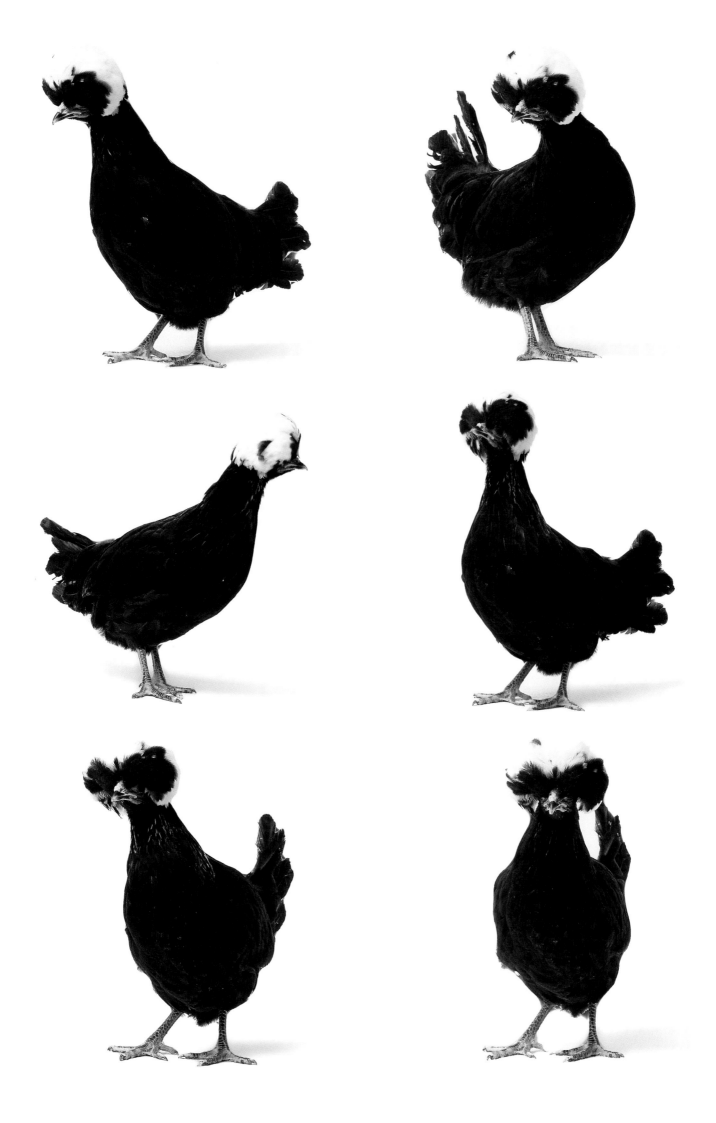

Egg nog with orange-flower water

For our grandmothers in times past this was a real magic potion.
There's nothing more effective to cure a cold than a good egg
nog, they would assure us! To get rid of a persistent cough?
Egg nog. Relieve toothache? Egg nog again. This recipe, handed
down from mother to daughter, was drunk in the evening at sunset.
We'll leave you to judge for yourself! You can, of course, replace the
orange-flower water with rum.

Serves 4
Preparation: 10 minutes
Cooking: 5 minutes
Degree of difficulty:

2½ cups (600 ml) milk
4 extra-fresh egg yolks
4 tsp. superfine sugar
2 tsp. orange-flower water
Finely pared orange zest, to decorate

Pour the milk into a saucepan and heat gently until hot.

Meanwhile, put the egg yolks, sugar, and orange-flower water
in a large bowl and whisk thoroughly until the mixture becomes
white and creamy.

Gradually whisk in the hot milk, until smooth and well mixed.
Pour the egg nog into cups or mugs, decorate with orange zest,
and serve immediately.

Egg nog with orange-flower water

When Renard talks of hens...!

"Feet together, she jumps down from the henhouse, as soon as they open the door.

She's an ordinary hen, modestly adorned, who never lays eggs of gold.

Dazzled by light, she takes a few steps, wobbly, in the courtyard.

The first thing she sees is the pile of cinders where, every morning, she likes to frolic.

She rolls in them, wets herself, and wings fluttering rapidly, feathers puffed up, she shakes out the nighttime fleas.

Then she goes and drinks from the hollow dish filled by the last shower.

She only drinks water.

She drinks in small gulps and straightens her neck, balanced on the edge of the dish.

Next, she searches for scarce food.

The mixed herbs are hers, and the insects and scattered seeds.

She pecks and pecks again, untiringly.

From time to time, she stops.

Standing in her Phrygian cap, beady-eyed, her jabot most appealing, she listens first with one ear, then the other.

And, sure now that there's nothing new, returns to her quest.

She lifts her stiff feet high, like those who suffer from gout. She spreads her webbed feet wide and puts them down carefully, noiselessly.

It's as if she were walking barefoot."

Jules Renard

Houdan

identity tag

Famous in the 18th century for her excellent meat, then gradually abandoned, this hen was born in Houdan (Ile-de-France) and is now making a big comeback on French farms.

cock: 6 lb. (3 kg)
hen: 5 lb. (2.5 kg)
egg: 2½ oz. (65 g), white
varieties: black, mottled, white...

155

Jura

Potato gratin with chicken stock

A warming "country" recipe, ideal in winter.

Serves 6
Preparation: 25 minutes
Cooking: 1 to 1¼ hours
Degree of difficulty:

1 garlic clove, peeled
Butter, for greasing
2 lb. (1 kg) potatoes
1¼ cups (300 ml) chicken stock
2 fresh thyme sprigs, finely chopped
7 oz. (200 g) comté (or gruyere)
  cheese, grated
Salt and freshly ground black pepper

Rub the inside of a shallow 10½ in. (26 cm) baking dish with the garlic clove, then grease the dish with a little butter. Peel the potatoes, wash and dry them in a cloth, then cut them into thin slices; season with salt and pepper. Lay the potato slices in closely overlapping rows in the gratin dish.

Pour the chicken stock over the potatoes, sprinkle the thyme over the top, and cover with grated cheese. Season with some more ground black pepper.

Place in a preheated 425°F (220°C) oven for 10 minutes. Reduce the oven temperature to 325°F (160°C) and cook for another 45 to 60 minutes, or until the potatoes are tender and the top is golden brown. Toward the end of the cooking time, you can cover the gratin with a sheet of parchment paper to prevent it from drying out, if desired.

Serve very hot. This dish is perfect served with a fresh herb salad or grilled sausages.

Potato gratin with
chicken stock

The hens of Mount Athos

Mount Athos, in Greece, is famous for its amazing architecture and its twenty monasteries. It is a place devoted to prayer and worship, and no "female" presence is tolerated within its walls; entry to the holy mountain is forbidden for "any female animal, any woman, any eunuch, and anyone with a smooth face"!

No female presence? Not quite, because there is one species which benefits from right of entry. It's the hen. Yes, hens live within the monastery precincts. And why this exception? Because the monks need egg yolks and shells to paint their famous frescoes and precious icons!

Java

identity tag

This very old bantam breed is said to come from the island of Java, hence her name. She was selected in England.

cock: 1 lb. 3 oz. (600 g)
hen: 1 lb. (500 g)
egg: 1 oz. (25 g), white
varieties: black, white, cuckoo...

General Dourakine's fat hen of Le Mans

"Jacques and Paul had eaten until that moment without saying a word. But on seeing the chicken, they finally recognized what they were eating.
'Ah! There's meat at last,' cried Paul.
'Meat?' repeated the General, indignantly. 'Where do you see meat, my boy?'

Jacques:
'There, General! In that dish. They're Aunt Elfy's chickens.'

The indignant General:
'My good woman, I beg of you, explain to the children that these are fat hens from Le Mans, the finest and most delicate that you can eat!'

Elfy, laughing:
'Do you think, General, that my chickens are not fine and delicate!'
'Your chickens! Your chickens!' repeated the General, containing his indignation.
'My child, the creatures you are eating are specially fattened up roasting chickens, their flesh is succulent [...].'

Elfy:
'What about my chickens?'

The General:
'What the devil! Your chickens are dry, blackened, miserable creatures who bear not the remotest resemblance to these fat and admirable hens.' "

Comtesse de Ségur, The Inn of the Guardian Angel

La Flèche

identity tag

She was already well known and much appreciated in the 15th century. Rabelais loved this hen because she was still, in his day, "force-fed with aromatic pellets." This breed is famous for the capons she produces.

cock: 7 to 8 lb.
(3.5 to 4 kg)
hen: 6 to 7 lb.
(3 to 3.5 kg)
egg: 3 oz. (70 g), white
varieties: black, blue,
cuckoo, white...

Saffron chicken quenelles

Bresse

Saffron chicken quenelles

Knödels are little balls of stuffing bound together and shaped with a spoon. Despite their German name, which was the origin of "quenelles," this delicate dish seems to have been inherited from Florentine cooking. It is difficult to say where quenelles themselves really came from. They can be found in almost all European countries and even in Asia (China). However, it was with the famous pike or chicken quenelles that they truly achieved distinction.

Makes about 15 quenelles (Serves 4 to 6)
Preparation: 25 minutes/Cooking: 45 minutes

Degree of difficulty:

2 cups (500 ml) chicken stock
½ tsp. saffron strands
2 skinless boneless chicken breasts,
  about 4 oz. (125 g) each
1 cup (250 ml) milk
5½ tbsp. (100 g) butter, diced
Grated nutmeg, to taste
1¼ cups (175 g) all-purpose flour
2 large eggs
Salt and freshly ground black pepper
Fresh parsley sprigs, to garnish

Pour the chicken stock into a saucepan, add the saffron strands, and heat gently until boiling. Add the chicken, cover, and simmer for about 20 minutes, or until the chicken is cooked and tender. Remove the chicken using a slotted spoon, finely chop the meat, and set aside. Strain and reserve the chicken stock.

Put the milk and butter into a saucepan. Season with salt and pepper and sprinkle in a little grated nutmeg. Heat gently, and as soon as the butter has melted, add the flour all at once. Stir well with a spatula, then cook gently for at least 5 minutes, stirring. Remove the pan from the heat and stir for a few more minutes.

Add 1 egg to the pan and stir well until it is completely absorbed into the flour mixture. Add the remaining egg and proceed in the same way. Finally, add the chopped chicken and mix everything together well.

Shape the mixture into quenelles using 2 spoons dipped in hot water. Gently reheat the chicken stock in a pan until it is hot. Carefully place the quenelles in the hot stock and poach them gently for a few minutes. As soon as they rise up to the surface, drain them and place in serving bowls. Cover with the saffron-flavored stock, garnish with parsley sprigs, and serve.

Vendée

Chicken in a salt crust

This is an old recipe which was prepared by people who worked on the salt marshes.
The method of cooking in salt is very healthy and quite spectacular and the chicken can be carried directly to the table for serving. Then you can ask your guests to break open the salt crust themselves and all breathe in the delicious aromas released from it!

Serves 4 to 6
Preparation: 10 minutes/Cooking: 1¼ hours

Degree of difficulty:

1 garlic clove
1 fresh thyme sprig
1 oven-ready chicken, about 3 lb. (1.5 kg)
About 6 lb. (3 kg) coarse sea salt
Freshly ground black pepper

Put the garlic clove and thyme sprig inside the cavity of the chicken and season with a little black pepper. Put a 1½ in. (3.5 cm) layer of salt over the bottom of an ovenproof cast iron baking pan. Place the chicken on this bed of salt and then cover it completely with more salt.

Place in a preheated 425°F (220°C) oven for about 1¼ hours. The salt will gradually form a hard crust around the chicken.

Remove the baking pan from the oven and leave it to stand for a few minutes.

Break the salt crust open and your chicken will appear, steaming and perfectly cooked!

Carve the chicken and serve it with steamed vegetables, sprinkled with a little salt.

Chicken in a salt crust

The philosophizing hen!

Philosophers don't only say daft things, they sometimes write them too.

A good example is the scholarly dispute over which came first, the chicken or the egg.

"It was the chicken!" argue some, because she laid the egg.

"Not at all!" cluck others, disapprovingly, "it was the egg that came first because the chicken came out of the egg!"

If you want our opinion...

"We can do without that!" says the little Taoist hen.

It's a bit facile, your story of the philosophizing hen! Don't you think?

Dutch bantam

identity tag

Originally from Germany, this bantam breed is quite rare and still remains a curiosity for many poultry breeders.

cock: 1 lb. 7 oz. (700 g)
hen: 1 lb. 3 oz. (600 g)
egg: 1 oz. (25 g)
varieties: golden, partridge...

One plus one equals eggs!

The number of eggs laid by a hen has always given rise to learned and scholarly disputes. Is it better to have hens that lay eggs in odd or even numbers? A real brain-teaser... some assure us that if eggs are laid in odd numbers, it brings bad luck. Others argue that nothing is more eggs'acerbatingly inauspicious than an even number. According to the elder Pliny, celebrated naturalist and Roman writer:

Hens should hatch an odd number of eggs, thirteen being the ideal number. For, in his view, an even number brings bad luck and the eggs then only produce... cockerels! A disaster for the species!

A proverb will serve (temporarily) to close this war of numbers with its ludicrous arithmetic: "You should never count your chickens before they're hatched!"

Phoenix

identity tag

Very old ornamental
breed, said to have
originated in Japan.

cock: 4 to 5 lb.
(2 to 2.5 kg)
hen: 3 to 4 lb.
(1.5 to 2 kg)
egg: 1½ oz. (45 g),
creamy white
varieties: silver or
golden duck-wing,
white...

Japan

Japanese-style rolled omelet

The Japanese have succeeded in squaring the circle... Once cooked, the Japanese omelet is finshed in a square "pan"! It enables them to make a delicious garnish for sushi.
In Japan, this is traditionally served for breakfast with miso soup.

Serves 6
Preparation: 5 minutes,
  plus standing
Cooking: 10 minutes

Degree of difficulty:

8 eggs
2 tsp. granulated sugar
2 tsp. Japanese soy sauce
1 tsp. mirin (Japanese sweet
  rice wine)
1 tbsp. sunflower oil
Salt, to taste

Break the eggs into a large bowl, add the sugar, soy sauce, mirin, and salt, and whisk together well using a fork.

Heat the oil in a frying pan and pour in one-third of the beaten egg mixture. Cook for a few minutes until the mixture is set and lightly browned, then roll it to one side of the pan.

Pour the second third of the egg mixture into the pan and, as before, let it cook for a few minutes.

Roll this second omelet around the first one. Repeat this procedure again for a third time with the remaining egg mixture and roll this omelet around the other two.

Place the omelet in a tea towel or on a little mat of plaited bamboo (maki-su), press lightly to give it a nice rectangular shape, then leave it like this for about 10 minutes.

Cut the omelette into slices and serve it cold.

Japanese-style rolled omelette

Korea

Steamed chicken flans

Inspired by a traditional Korean dish, this recipe is equally tasty made with prawns or beef. If you don't possess a steamer, cook these little flans in a water bath.

Serves 4
Preparation: 15 minutes, plus standing/Cooking: 15 minutes
Degree of difficulty:

3 oz. (75 g) cooked skinless boneless chicken breast,
  finely chopped
2 tbsp. soy sauce
1 tbsp. chopped fresh coriander leaves
4 eggs
2 tbsp. chopped scallions
1 tbsp. rice wine (or dry white wine)
Salt and freshly ground black pepper

Put the chicken into a bowl, add the soy sauce and chopped coriander, stir to mix, then cover and leave in a cool place for 20 minutes.

Whisk the eggs in a bowl, season lightly with salt and pepper, then stir in the scallions, wine, and chicken mixture.

Divide the mixture equally between 4 ramekin dishes. Put the ramekins into a steamer basket, cover, and steam over a pan of simmering water for about 15 minutes, or until lightly set. Serve immediately.

Chicken breasts with rice and soy sauce

This recipe is traditionally served in individual terracotta bowls.

Serves 4
Preparation: 10 minutes/Cooking: 20 minutes
Degree of difficulty:

2½ cups (600 ml) chicken stock
5 tbsp. Japanese soy sauce
2 tbsp. mirin (Japanese sweet rice wine)
2 skinless boneless chicken breasts,
  about 4 oz. (125 g) each, diced
4 eggs
4 scallions, cut into thin strips
2 cups (250 g) cooked hot rice
Salt, to taste

Pour the stock into a saucepan, add the soy sauce and mirin, and heat over fairly high heat until boiling.

As soon as the stock comes to a boil, add the chicken, then reduce the heat, cover, and cook gently for about 10 minutes, or until the chicken is cooked and tender.

Break the eggs into a bowl, add a little salt, then whisk the eggs with a fork. Pour this mixture into the hot stock, add the scallions, and cook gently for 4 to 5 minutes.

Spoon the hot rice into serving bowls, remove the diced chicken and cooked eggs from the pan using a slotted spoon, and lay them on top of the rice. Spoon the stock over the top, if desired. Serve.

Chicken breasts with
rice and soy sauce

Japan

Mini Japanese kebabs

The Japanese love yakitori, these little kebabs that are cooked on a grill and served with an aperitif or as a starter with a glass of sake.
Use Japanese soy sauce (a mixture of soy beans and fermented wheat) for these chicken kebabs, not Chinese soy sauce which has a very different flavor!

Serves 4
Preparation: 15 minutes
Cooking: 15 minutes

Degree of difficulty:

1 lb. (500 g) skinless boneless chicken
  thighs, chopped
4 tsp. Japanese soy sauce
2 tsp. mirin (Japanese sweet
  rice wine)
2 tsp. granulated sugar
1½ tsp. cornstarch
Salt, to taste
Chopped fresh chives, to garnish

Put the chicken in a bowl, add the soy sauce, mirin, sugar, and cornstarch and mix well, then form the mixture into small balls of equal size.

Bring a large saucepan of water to the boil, then immerse the balls in the boiling water for 3 minutes. Drain the chicken balls thoroughly, then thread them onto short wooden kebab sticks or skewers.

Put the kebabs on a rack in a grill pan and cook under a preheated hot grill until cooked and lightly browned all over, turning occasionally. Season with a little salt, garnish with chopped chives, and serve with a bowl of cooked rice.

Mini Japanese kebabs

Feathers of every hue!

Whether they're simple farm chickens or luxury varieties, hens have become queens of the farmyard. Breeders have long tried to solve the mystery of their plumage. One popular belief said that if an egg started to hatch on Good Friday, the plumage of the bird which emerged from it would change color each year.

The Limousin cockerel is known as the fishing cock, and is famous on account of his little blue feathers with which artificial flies are made for trout fishing. And for centuries, milliners used hen and cockerel feathers to decorate hats with.

As for the courtesans of the 1900s, those exotic birds celebrated by painters and writers, they used not chicken but ostrich feathers!

Brief history of the bantam hen!

Contrary to popular belief, the bantam is definitely not a reduced version of a full-sized hen. As proof of this, the bantam also exists in the wild, and certain miniature breeds, like the Peking bantam, don't even have an equivalent large breed!

The Chinese, who were lovers of miniatures, were the first to breed them and they were greatly venerated. The Egyptians, Greeks, and Romans were also familiar with bantam hens but they held them in low esteem.

In the West, Marco Polo was one of the first to sing their praises. His description of the Negro-silk (see p.108) impressed itself on people's minds. But it was particularly from the 18th century onwards, with the crossbreeding carried out by Sir John Sebright, that the bantam breeds found favor with both breeders and the public. Since the end of the 19th century, breeders have tried to outdo one another in the patience and care they lavish on giving each main breed its equivalent bantam version. Sometimes this can take more than thirty years.

Sebright

identity tag

Created in England in
1800 by Sir John Sebright,
an English Member of
Parliament who was
passionate about
poultry breeding.
One of the most beautiful
ornamental breeds.

cock: 1 lb. 3 oz. (600 g)
hen: 1 lb. (500 g)
egg: 1¼ oz. (30 to 35 g),
lightly tinted white
varieties: silver, golden,
lemon...

Nasr Eddin Hodja's chicken broth!

One day Nasr Eddin Hodja was given a hen by one of his neighbors.

"Let's eat it together," suggested Nasr Eddin. And straight away he prepared a succulent meal.

Two days later, an unknown visitor knocked at Nasr Eddin's door.

"I'm the neighbor of the man who gave you the hen!"

"Come in, my friend, and share my meal!" suggested Nasr Eddin.

And the man ate with a hearty appetite.

The next day, another stranger knocked at Nasr Eddin's door.

"I'm the neighbor of the neighbor of the man who gave you a hen!"

"Come in, friend," suggested Hodja, "and share my meal."

And the man ate with a hearty appetite.

The following day, yet another stranger knocked at Nasr Eddin's door.

"I am the neighbor of the neighbor of the neighbor of the man who gave you a hen."

"Come in," suggested Nasr Eddin again, "and share my meal."

And he served him a bowlful of hot water with just a bit of fat floating in it.

"Is that the way you show me hospitality?" asked the guest, angrily.

"I've served you the broth of the broth of the broth from the hen that my neighbor gave me!"

Sultan

identity tag

cock: 5 lb. (2.5 kg)
hen: 4 lb. (2 kg)
egg: 2 oz. (55 g), white
variety: white

Chicken soup with rice and lemon

Chicken soup with rice and lemon

This recipe is prepared for the Orthodox Easter. The traditional *avgolémono soupa* is a chicken stock thickened with a mixture of egg and lemon, which gives it a delicate, slightly acid flavor. The Greeks also make fish, lamb, and beef soups in the same way.

Serves 4 to 6
Preparation: 15 minutes/Cooking: 20 to 25 minutes
Degree of difficulty:

2 carrots, thinly sliced
1 celery stalk, finely chopped
4 cups (1 l) chicken stock
2/3 cup (100 g) long grain white rice
2 eggs
Juice of 1 lemon
2 tbsp. chopped fresh parsley
Salt and white pepper

Put the carrots and celery into a saucepan. Add the stock, then bring gently to a boil. As soon as it comes to a boil, add the rice, then reduce the heat and simmer, uncovered, about 15 to 20 minutes or until the rice is cooked and tender. Remove the pan from the heat.

Break the eggs into a bowl and whisk them lightly, then gradually add the lemon juice a drop at a time, whisking continuously. Whisk in 2 tbsp. of the hot stock.

Add the egg mixture to the rice and whisk to mix. Add salt and pepper to taste, then add the chopped parsley and serve at once.

Chicken couscous

There are a thousand and one ways to prepare couscous. Rather than start an argument, we'll content ourselves with suggesting this very simple version for you to make.

Serves 4 to 6
Preparation: 25 minutes/Cooking: 55 minutes
Degree of difficulty:

3 cups (500 g) couscous
1 cup (250 ml) lukewarm water, salted
1 tbsp. olive oil
4 carrots, sliced
3 zucchini, sliced
3 turnips, cut into large cubes
2 celery stalks, chopped
1 garlic clove, peeled
1 small oven-ready chicken, about 2½ lb. (1.25 kg), cut up
2 tbsp. chopped fresh coriander leaves
5 tbsp. (65 g) butter, diced
1 tsp. harissa paste
4 oz. (125 g) dried chickpeas, cooked until tender, drained and kept warm
Salt and freshly ground black pepper

Put the couscous into a bowl, add the measured lukewarm water, and mix well, then add the oil and stir to mix.

Fluff up the couscous with a fork to stop it sticking together and put it in the top section of a couscous steamer.

Put 1 prepared carrot, 1 zucchini, 1 turnip, 1 celery stalk, and the garlic clove into the bottom of the couscous steamer. Season with salt and pepper, then pour in 8 cups (2 l) of water, cover, and bring to a boil. Fit in the basket containing the couscous over the bottom of the steamer, cover, and steam for 15 minutes.

Remove the garlic clove and crush the flesh. Put the chicken pieces in the lower compartment of the couscous steamer, add salt to taste, then add the remaining prepared vegetables, the crushed garlic, and chopped coriander. Give the couscous a good stir with a fork, then cover and steam for another 15 minutes.

Again stir the couscous with a fork, then cover and cook for another 15 to 20 minutes.

Turn out the couscous into a deep serving dish, add the butter, and stir gently to mix. Roll the couscous between your fingers to make sure each grain is well separated. Cover, keep warm, and set aside.

Make sure the chicken is cooked and tender, then remove it from the stock together with the vegetables, cover, and keep warm.

Strain the stock which is in the bottom of the cooking pot, remove 1 ladleful of the stock and mix it with the harissa paste. Set aside. Ladle the remaining stock into serving bowls.

Serve the cooked chicken pieces and vegetables with the couscous, chickpeas, stock, and harissa sauce.

Chicken couscous

Greece

Tiropitès with egg, feta, and coriander

Tiropitès are little pastries stuffed with meat or egg. They are sometimes sweet, in which case they are decorated with almonds or cream... In Greece, you can buy them from street traders.

Serves 4
Preparation: 15 minutes/Cooking: 15 to 20 minutes
Degree of difficulty:

4 eggs, beaten
7 oz. (200 g) feta cheese, crumbled
2 tbsp. chopped fresh coriander leaves
4 sheets of phyllo or puff pastry
Salt and freshly ground black pepper

Lightly grease a baking sheet and set aside. Mix the eggs, feta cheese, and chopped coriander together in a bowl. Season with a little salt and pepper.

Dampen the phyllo sheets with a little water using your fingers. Take one phyllo sheet and place one quarter of the feta stuffing mixture in the center of the phyllo. Fold the pastry edges over the filling to make it into a rectangular, triangular, or cigar shape. Set aside.

Repeat with the remaining phyllo sheets and feta filling to make a total of 4 pastries.

Place the pastries on the prepared baking sheet and place in a preheated 400°F (200°C) oven for 15 to 20 minutes, or until cooked and lightly browned.

Serve immediately.

Morocco

Chicken tagine with prunes, honey, and almonds

A tagine is a hollow, glazed terracotta dish surmounted by a conical cover. You find it primarily in North African countries. Tagine is also the name of a stew, for which the ingredients vary according to country and custom: You can have tagines of fish, vegetables, meat or fruit...
This recipe can also be prepared in a heavy bottomed stewpot and served sprinkled with sesame seeds.

Serves 4 to 6
Preparation: 15 minutes, plus soaking/Cooking: 1 hour 5 minutes
Degree of difficulty:

5 oz. (150 g) prunes
2 tbsp. olive oil
1 small oven-ready chicken, about 2½ lb. (1.25 kg), cut up
2 onions, chopped
1 tbsp. ground cinnamon
2 tbsp. honey
1 cup (250 ml) chicken stock
1 cup (100 g) blanched whole almonds
Salt and freshly ground black pepper

Put the prunes in a bowl, cover them with warm water, then leave them to soak for at least 30 minutes. Drain the prunes and set aside.

Heat 1 tbsp. oil in a stewpot or tagine. Add the chicken pieces and cook until browned all over, turning occasionally. Remove the chicken from the pot, set aside, and keep warm.

Heat the remaining oil in the pot or tagine, add the onions, and sauté until lightly browned all over. Return the chicken to the pot, sprinkle with cinnamon, and season with salt and pepper.

Add the honey and stir to mix, then add the chicken stock. Cover, bring slowly to a boil, then simmer gently for about 20 minutes.

Add the prunes and almonds, cover, and cook very gently for another 25 minutes, or until the chicken is cooked and tender.

Taste and adjust the seasoning, if necessary, and serve hot.

chicken tagine with prunes
honey, and almonds

Chicken stuffed with rice,
lamb, and cinnamon

Chicken stuffed with rice, lamb, and cinnamon

This traditional dish is delicious with fattouche (a salad made up of cucumber, mint, fresh herbs...) and a bowl of Lebanese-style rice. The stuffing is very tasty.

Serves 4 to 6
Preparation: 40 minutes
Cooking: 1 to 1¼ hours

Degree of difficulty:

¾ cup (200 ml) chicken stock
¼ cup (50 g) long grain white rice
1 tbsp. sunflower oil
1 onion, chopped
5 oz. (150 g) lamb, minced or ground
¼ cup (50 g) pine nuts
2 pinches of ground cinnamon
1 small oven-ready chicken,
  about 2½ lb. (1.25 kg)
Salt and freshly ground black pepper
Cucumber slices and chopped herbs,
  to garnish

Pour the chicken stock into a saucepan and bring to a boil. Add the rice, reduce the heat, then cover and simmer gently for about 15 to 20 minutes, or until the rice is cooked. Drain well and set aside.

Heat the oil in a frying pan, add the onion, and sauté until lightly browned all over. Add the lamb and cook until seared all over, stirring occasionally. Remove the onions and lamb from the pan, place in a dish, and set aside.

Add the pine nuts to the frying pan and cook gently until toasted all over. Add to the lamb mixture together with the cooked rice, cinnamon, and salt and pepper. Mix well.

Season the inside of the chicken with a little black pepper, then spoon the lamb mixture into the chicken cavity. Truss up the end of the chicken with a needle and butcher's twine.

Place the chicken in an ovenproof dish, season with salt and pepper, then place in a preheated 400°F (200°C) oven about 1 to 1¼ hours or until the chicken is cooked and tender. Baste the chicken regularly with the cooking juices during cooking so that the meat stays tender.

Serve immediately, garnished with cucumber slices and chopped herbs.

Appendices

"Proper" chicken stock

Every family is convinced that it has the "proper" recipe for chicken stock! They've inherited it from a grandmother, who already had it from her grandmother, who got it from… and so on and so on, from time immemorial.

This tradition of the old family secret (a bit like the secret of Alphonse Daudet's miller, Maître Cornille, in *Lettres de mon Moulin,* which is really more of a bluff!) inspires us to share our own recipe with you. The "proper" one, of course!

Serves 6
Preparation: 15 minutes
Cooking: 2½ hours

Degree of difficulty:

1 oven-ready chicken,
   about 3 lb. (1.5 kg)
4 small carrots, left whole
2 leeks, washed and thickly sliced
¼ celery root, cut into chunks
1 onion, cut into quarters
Small bunch of fresh parsley
1 fresh thyme sprig
8 black peppercorns
Salt, to taste
Chopped fresh parsley, to serve

Put the chicken into a large, heavy bottomed pot, add the prepared vegetables, bunch of parsley, thyme, and peppercorns. Cover with cold water, add some salt, and bring to a boil.

Reduce the heat, then cover and simmer for about 2 hours or until the chicken is cooked and tender. Check to see whether the chicken is cooked by piercing the thickest part of the flesh with the point of a knife - the juices should run clear.

Remove the chicken from the cooking pot and use as required. Strain the stock and skim off the fat with a spoon.

Serve the broth very hot, sprinkled with chopped parsley.

"Proper" chicken stock

Contents by recipe

Table of hens

Bibliography

ABC of Poultry Raising: A Complete Guide for the Beginner or Expert, J.H. Florea (Dover Publications).

Aesop: The Complete Fables, Aesop et al.

Bantams in Colour, Michael Roberts et al. (Gold Cockerel Books).

Big Book of Garden Hens, Francine Raymond (Kitchen Garden).

British Large Fowl, Michael Roberts, John Tarren (Gold Cockerel Books).

British Poultry Standards, Victoria Roberts (Blackwell Science, UK).

Chickens In Your Backyard: A Beginner's Guide, Rick Luttmann (Rodale Press).

The Complete Book of Raising Livestock and Poultry, Katie Thear, Alistair Fraser (eds.) (Pan Paperback).

Extraordinary Chickens, Stephen Green-Armytage (Harry N. Abrams, Inc).

Home Poultry Keeping, Geoffrey Eley (A & C Black).

Natural Poultry Keeping: Free Range and Other Systems, J. Batty (Beech Publishing House).

Old Poultry Breeds, Fred Hams (Shire Publications Ltd.).

Acknowledgments

To Pascale and Jacques Nutall, for their welcome
and invaluable help in producing the photos.

To their hens, who knew how to pose like real film stars!

If you are going near Kérès Farm in Brittany, do not hesitate to pay them a visit.

Tel: 0033 (0)2 96 47 00 42 . http://perso.wanadoo.fr/ferme-de-keres . keres@wanadoo.fr

To John Clikmann for allowing us to photograph
his magnificent Negro-silk hens for page 109.
http://perso.wanadoo.fr/aristosoie

To our mothers, Arlette and Rosine, for their incomparable know-how in the kitchen.

Other collaborators in the production of this book are:

Gérard Ciprès for producing the recipes.
Véronique Dussidour and Fella Saïdi-Tournoux for reading, re-reading and correcting.
Francis Delbassez for photo-engraving at Euresys in Baisieux.

First published by Marabout, an imprint of Hachette-Livre,
43 Quai de Grenelle, Paris 75905, Cedex 15, France
© 2001 Marabout, Paris.
Text and recipes © Laurence & Gilles Laurendon
Photographs of recipes © Akiko Ida
Photographs of hens © Laurent Parrault
All rights reserved

English translation rights © 2002 by Ici La Press

Printed and bound in Singapore

Published by Ici La Press
694 Main St. South
Woodbury, CT 06798
www.icilapress.com

ISBN 1-931605-13-0